A Lawn Chair Gardener's GUIDE

TO A BALANCED LIFE AND WORLD

Dawn Viola Pape

Good Green Life Publishing

St. Paul, Minnesota
2016

GOOD GREEN LIFE
— publishing —

P.O. Box 74

Circle Pines, MN 55014-1793

While the author and publisher have made every effort to provide accurate website addresses at the time of publication, they do not assume responsibility for errors, or for changes that occur after publication. Further, the author and publsiher do not have any control over, and does not assume any responsibility for, the third-party websites or their content.

All photos and illustrations were taken or created by the author with these exceptions (in the order of appearance in book): bicycle, blueberries, rabbit, deer, three-legged stool. These photos were purchased from Shutterstock.

A Lawn Chair Gardener's Guide to a Balanced Life and a More Balanced World eBook edition April 2012 ISBN: 978-0-9851877-0-5
A Lawn Chair Gardener's Guide to a Balanced Life and a More Balanced World paperback edition March 2013 ISBN: 978-0-9851877-1-2
A Lawn Chair Gardener's Guide to a Balanced Life and World paperback edition April 2013 ISBN: 978-0-9851877-2-9
A Lawn Chair Gardener's Guide to a Balanced Life and World paperback edition February 2014 (second printing) ISBN: 978-0-9851877-2-9
A Lawn Chair Gardener's Guide to a Balanced Life and World paperback edition January 2016 (third printing) ISBN: 978-0-9851877-2-9

PRINTED IN THE UNITED STATES OF AMERICA

Dedication

For Mason and Maxwell, my inspiration.
May you live in a world where functional yards are the status quo.

Acknowledgements

Thank you to my unbelievably wonderful husband, Kevin.

A warm thanks also to my family and friends who offered me encouragement and suggestions—Jan Dubats, Dena DeGroat, Sue McKendry, Elizabeth Beckman, Matt Lilley, Annie Dubats, Maureen Casperson and Kelly Tokay and all of my Minnesota Rover Friends.

Contents

chapter one

Lawn Chair Gardening

The Emerging New Normal in Yard Care

Introduction

Picture yourself relaxing in your yard on a perfect summer day, breathing in the divine fragrance of your herbs. You have plenty of time to just sit and enjoy watching the birds and butterflies flitting about your flowers. You appreciate the orchestra of beneficial insects, which not only provide the background music, but also double as the patrol squad, keeping the bad bugs at bay. Maybe you're having some blissful alone time or perhaps you're sharing your favorite beverage with a few of your best friends.

Now envision simply stepping out to the garden to pick a delicious, healthy salad. Your kids are excited and proud to eat their vegetables because the vegetables truly are *their* vegetables; they helped plant, water, and pick them.

What if abundant community gardens grew in the middle of every neighborhood and extra produce were shared with people in need?

Imagine the healthful impacts of eating fresh, locally grown produce and getting exercise without working out at a gym.

Consider how much healthier the planet would be if we reduced our carbon footprints by about one-third[1] just by eating locally and seasonally.

How would it be if families and friends bonded through shared, outdoor experiences? And, rather than spending disturbing amounts of time indoors, in front of TV or computer screens, kids ran and played outside and reveled in the beauty of each season. What if kids were allowed to get bored and watch insects?

I believe all of these things are possible through what I call "lawn chair gardening."

What if, before each meal, we got in the habit of thanking the pollinating insects that make our food possible?

What is Lawn Chair Gardening?

You might be thinking that a lawn chair gardener is the same as a lazy gardener, but that's not what I mean. To me, the term "lawn chair gardener" refers to gardeners who have well-rounded lives and take a balanced approach to gardening. Even when I was single with no children, I didn't want to take the time to cater to the special care requirements of certain plants. Nor did I want to be bothered by needy annuals that demanded daily watering and guilted me into limiting my vacations so they wouldn't die of thirst in my absence. In my world, plants shouldn't require lining up a caretaker for when you go out of town.

Lawn chair gardeners take use natural processes to their advantage. For example, instead of using pesticides, plant native plants to bring in the beneficial insects. As my husband puts it, lawn chair gardeners are pleased with 80 percent of the returns for 20 percent of the labor. If you have to create a garden from scratch, it will require some up-front work, but after the gardens are estab-

---

1   Eatlowcarbon.org

lished, the workload should be as much as you would like it to be—not as much as the garden demands of you. I understand that you might want to maintain relationships with family, friends, kids, work, and perhaps (gasp!) even develop other hobbies!

The flip side of the lawn chair gardener is the obsessive gardener. Perhaps you've read about these gardeners in your local newspaper or run-the-gamut home magazine. I greedily devour each word of these articles, soaking in the featured gardener's experience. As the story unfolds, it is revealed that the gardeners either spent an exorbitant amount of money redesigning their garden three times over the past 20 years and/or they spend an average of four hours per day gardening. At that point, I put the article down, look out my sunny kitchen window and ponder, "Who are these people?"

I compare these gardeners to Hollywood celebrities, because, to me, their gardens are as unattainable as a Hollywood star's perfectly sculpted body. I dismiss the garden with, "Sure, who wouldn't have a perfect garden if you had four hours a day to spend on it?" I bet that photo of their garden in the article is air-brushed too. I also wonder how these awe-inspiring gardeners find time to socialize, do the laundry, take care of their kids, shop, prepare meals, and maybe even—heaven forbid—go to work. Many jobs require a person to be at work during prime gardening hours.

Perhaps some day I will have the free time to be an obsessive gardener and grow every morsel of produce my family consumes. But, right now, there are plenty of days when I am satisfied with getting four hours of sleep at night. I am 41 years old, I have a three-year old and an infant, and I work part-time. To boot, I live in the Midwest (zone 4), where the growing season is a sprint and our planting palette is comparable to the 24-count box of crayons—not the huge box with the pencil sharpener on the back enjoyed in the warmer regions that are typically featured in magazines.

The Purpose of this Book

This book is for gardeners with an interest in a balanced life and a more balanced world. It's for people who enjoy spending time outside and hope to squeeze in a couple hours per week (or month) to garden. This book is also for people who want their garden to make a positive impact on the world by creating eco-friendly yards that provide food and habitat for both people and wildlife.

I have written this book for beginning and experienced gardeners who are interested in venturing into the world of edible and native plants using methods that are beneficial to the environment. On the following pages, I will lay out reasons why gardening with the environment in mind makes sense as well as offer practical tips for planning, planting, and tending native and edible gardens. Finally, I offer 40 simple recipes on how to use your garden bounty and instructions on how to freeze your surplus. This book is not necessarily meant for the perfectionist who delights in doctoring dahlias. It is for the average Joe or Jodi who realizes there are personal, economic, and ecological benefits to lawn chair gardening and is looking for some guidance. Since numerous encyclopedias and reference guides are already available, I am not trying to reinvent them. When specific issues pop up, please use resources or visit the website of your local university extension. Some of my favorite references and tools are listed throughout the chapters and on my website to aid you in answering very specific questions.

There's little risk in becoming overly proud of one's garden because gardening by its very nature is humbling. It has a way of keeping you on your knees.

- Joanne R. Barwick, Readers Digest, 1993

My aim is to remove some of the perceived complexity from gardening and to open people's minds to the new gardening possibilities in their own yards. As much as I enjoy my volunteer title as a "Master Gardener" through the University of Minnesota Extension Service, I am certainly not claiming to be a master of all things garden-related. The longer I garden, the more I realize how much I have yet to learn.

Though an old man, I am but a young gardener.

-Thomas Jefferson

Another key reason I am writing this book is that I see gardening as a way to mend some of the ills in society in a non-preachy, proactive way. What you do in your own yard sets a quiet example of the values you want to see in your community and across the globe.

The nice thing about being a lawn chair gardener is that you can choose what you'd like to do. For example, do you think starting your own seeds sounds like too much work? If it doesn't sound fun, just buy plants instead. There is no shame in doing only what interests you or what you have time for and there will be no judgment from this lawn chair gardener.

chapter two

The Eternal Quest

Finding Personal Balance

The Quest for Balance

FINDING BALANCE IS CENTRAL TO A HAPPY LIFE, and people all over the world have been incorporating moderation and balance into their teachings for thousands of years. In ancient Greece, "nothing in excess," or, stated in the positive, "all things in moderation" was inscribed upon the temple of Apollo at Delphi. In Taoism, moderation is considered a key part of personal development and is one of the three jewels of Taoist thought. It is believed that by maintaining balance, one achieves a more natural state, faces less resistance in life, and recognizes limits. The tricky part about finding balance is that life keeps moving, changing and throwing you curve balls that force you to find new balance with each passing day.

Does gardening help facilitate balance? Or do you need to have balance in your life to find time to garden? The answer to both of these questions may be "yes." I find when I am balanced, my life flows gracefully, in harmony and rhythm. Opportunities fall into place. Conversations happen and needed information presents itself.

I am peaceful, tolerant of others, and more in tune with myself. I also tend to follow my intuitions and dreams that guide me down a path of life that feels sunny, comfortable, and stable. This creates contentment and happiness where nothing seems like a chore. A little of this, a little of that, it all blends together to form a complete, artful life—like a delicious meal, beautiful music, or a breathtaking mural.

Gardening for a Balanced Life

Like my buddy Bert (Einstein) said, you must keep moving to stay balanced. In doing so, you're not stuck on one thing that will lead to excessiveness in any area of your life. I think that's why gardening helps a person stay balanced—conditions and seasons in the garden are constantly changing, so you are forced to change and keep moving along with it.

"Life is like riding a bicycle. To keep your balance, you must keep moving."
- Albert Einstein

If you're reading this book, you probably have many interests and demands on your time and can't, or choose not to, putter and prune from sunrise to sunset. You are looking to round out your life. A portrait of a balanced life is often divided into seven main facets. Look at how nicely gardening fits into each of these seven areas, enriching and adding balance to a person's life.

Physical—Health

When you spend time in your garden breathing fresh air and getting exercise, you will probably sleep well. You will grow some of your own organic, not genetically modified food to cook so you will likely eat well too. Everyone knows exercise sleep and diet are pillars of good health.

Spiritual

Gardening is a spiritual outlet that nourishes the soul. For centuries, poets, musicians, artists, saints and philosophers rediscovered peace and inspiration in gardens and nature. I believe they can't all be wrong. They must be onto something.

After a long Midwestern winter, it's uplifting to see a new life emerge. Gardening also helps a person to be present, clearing the mind of troubles from the past and setting aside worries about the future, focusing only on the task at hand. This act is very restorative and meditative.

You have to believe in the future to plant a garden.
- Anonymous

Financial

In return for a small amount of manual labor, gardening can save you money on food. Especially if you start your garden from seeds, you can have a bounty all summer for the cost of one bag of groceries.

Lawn chair gardening can also save money on your water bill. The typical suburban lawn consumes 10,000 gallons of water above and beyond rainwater each year.[2] A vegetable garden does need some watering, but not as much as a lawn, and at

---

2   U.S. Environmental Protection Agency, http://www.epa.gov/greenhomes/Outdoor.htm (Dec 2012).

least you're eating the food. Native plants require no watering after their first season, because they establish themselves quickly and have long enough roots to find their own water.

Strong Relationships with Family and Community

In general, working together on projects strengthens relationships. Gardens continue to expand, grow, and change each year. That means the whole family can be involved in and bond over this ever evolving project. My aunt says she feels the most married when she and my uncle work together in the garden.

Incorporating kids into garden projects certainly strengthens your relationship with the children. But perhaps more importantly, it strengthens the child's relationship to the world. Connecting kids with nature and the seasons helps combat what Richard Louv describes in his book *Last Child in the Woods* as "nature deficit disorder." In a similar fashion, the documentary film *Play Again* explores how far removed kids are from the outdoors and the greater societal impacts of this reality. For example, did you know that most young children can name every Disney and/or cartoon character and store logo but not a single tree or flower? I find this fact disturbing, but very solvable if we commit to reuniting kids and the outdoors. We, as adults, can start by paying attention to the natural world and pointing it out to the children in our lives. An easy way to start is with tree names. There's only about twenty common trees to learn in Minnesota so it's really not that hard.

Gardens can connect you to your community through garden clubs, neighbors, community gardens, and charities where you can donate produce or even bouquets of flowers.

Mental—Emotional

As with any hobby, gardening keeps a person thinking and learning, developing new pathways in the brain. But not all hobbies have the added advantage of reducing stress. A number of studies have presented strong evidence that even three to five minutes of contact with nature can significantly decrease stress, reduce anger and fear, and increase pleasant feelings.[3,4,5,6]

From what I can surmise, the art of happiness has a few common threads. Happy people have lasting, healthy relationships. Happy people practice gratitude. Happy people live in the moment and enjoy people, places, and ordinary things they encounter everyday. Happy people also enjoy giving. The very act of giving multiplies happiness because acts of kindness and charity amplify a person's feeling of well-being. It just feels good to be able to do something nice for someone else.

As happiness is a way of life, so is gardening. Gardening puts the gardener in touch with the rhythms of the earth and supports eating locally and in harmony with the seasons. There is a time to sow, tend, and reap. Happy people have difficult times, but are able to bounce back because they know better times are probable. Just as gardeners have tough years when their crops flop and flowers fail to thrive, a gardener perseveres and plants a garden the following year with the hope that next year might be better. The act of planting a garden is optimistic.

As described earlier, you may choose to make your garden a family endeavor. But other times you may gleefully escape to your garden to have a little quiet time. Through experience, I have learned that it can be a wee bit frustrating to garden with a toddler. When my son was 22 months old, he "helped" me by pulling up all of the plants that we had just planted together. He said, "Back!" as he proudly "cleaned up," sticking all of the uprooted plants back into their pots.

---

3   Parsons R, Hartig T. Environmental Psycholphysiology. *In Handbook of Psychophysiology, 2nd ed.* (New York: Cambridge University Press, 2000), 815-46.
4   Ulrich RS. *Effects of Interior Design of Wellness: Theory and Recent Scientific Research.* (J Health Care Interior Design, 1991), 3(1): 97-109.
5   Ulrich RS. Effects of Gardens on Health Outcomes: Theory and Recent Scientific Research, *Healing Gardens*, (New York: John Wiley & Sons, 1999), 27-86.
6   Van den Berg A, Koole SL, Van der Wulp NY. *Environmental Preference and Restoration: How are They Related?* (J Environ Psychology 2003), 23(2): 135-46.

How Happy Are You?

Rate Your Life As A Whole

On a scale of 1-10, how good is your life when you step back and think about it? (A 10 represents the best possible life for you.)[7]

Evaluate Your Feelings

Now consider your feelings when you are in nature or in your garden. Does your garden bring about positive or negative feelings?

Positive Feelings	Negative Feelings
Joy	Sadness or Anger
Contentment	Worry
Grateful	Ungrateful
Wonder	Boredom
Hope	Depressed or Hopeless
Pride	Shame

Work

Gardening can give a person an increased sense of purpose and accomplishment. It's nice to have tasks in life that have a beginning, middle, and end to them like each year of gardening—especially where seasons are so defined like in the Midwest. Perhaps my favorite reason to gardening: my gardens give me a viable excuse to avoid my indoor chores on a beautiful day. I tell myself the dishes will be there when I get done, so I better take advantage of this weather!

Social/Leisure

Flower gardens are essential for pollination and bring delight to the senses. The lawn chair garden is the perfect place to relax and bring people together over a healthy, (at least partially) homegrown meal.

---

7   Joseph Smiley, Professor of Psychology, Emeritus, University of Illinois, Scales by Ed Diener. Source: Hadley Cantril's Self-Anchoring Striving Scale. Reference: Cantril, H. (1966). Pattern of human concerns. (New Brunswick, NJ: Rutgers University Press), http://www.scientificamerican.com/article.cfm?id=happiness-how-happy-are-you-quiz, (April 2013)

chapter three

Plotting to Change the World

Gardening for a More Balanced World

Let's break the cycle of boring expanses of lawns, starved soil and mundane shrubs that are maintained with gas lawn mowers and leaf blowers. - Rosalind Creasy

A "Tipping Point" for Lawns?

As Malcolm Gladwell explores in his book, *The Tipping Point*, social phenomena act as epidemics. Gladwell boils down his theory to three laws: the law of the few, the stickiness factor, and the law of context.

The "law of the few" is about the structure of our social network and how messages are passed through word of mouth. It classifies three important types of people who affect the rapid spread of messages through the network. These three types of people are connectors (socialites with many friends), mavens (trusted information gatherers), and salespeople (persuaders).

The "stickiness factor" is about the informational content and packaging of a message. Connections and the personal character of the people trying to spread a message can certainly help it spread, but if the message is not worth spreading, it doesn't go anywhere. The stickiness factor says that messages must be deemed worthy of being passed on.

The "law of context" is about the environment in which a message spreads. Social epidemics do not keep spreading if the geographic location where they are introduced is wrong or if the population is not mentally prepared for the message.

As I read that book, my mind wandered a bit to consider several safety and environmental norms that have "tipped" in the past few decades. Just think of all the things that were normal a generation ago that seem bizarre now. For example, when I grew up in the 1970s, it was common practice to put asphalt or concrete under monkey bars. Were our park workers and school grounds supervisors trying to weed out a few of us plaid-bell-bottom-pants-sporting kids? Wood chips or sand is the standard now.

Now, let's think about car seats. These restraining devices were almost unheard of back in the 1970s. Today, I bet most parents fasten in their kids to drive across a parking lot. Smoking is another example. Teachers used to smoke in elementary school classrooms. Now I doubt any schools allow smoking on the school grounds. It used to be acceptable to spread out your used oil on dirt roads to keep down the dust. Today most people realize this harms the soil and can contaminate groundwater. And, how about littering? Some readers might remember the TV public service announcement featuring a crying Native American, "Iron Eyes Cody," saddened by all the litter. This campaign along with Woodsy Owl's, "Give a Hoot, Don't Pollute" slogan helped to tip our society to view littering as unacceptable.

Time will tell if people are open to changing their habits and incorporating alterna-

Anything else you're interested in is not going to happen if you can't breathe the air and drink the water. Don't sit this one out. Do something. You are by accident of fate alive at an absolutely critical moment in the history of our planet.
- Carl Sagan

tive landscaping and if "lawn chair gardening" is sticky enough to spread through social networks. My hope is that when my kids are grown up, having a purely aesthetic yard with only grass and ornamental plants that provide no food or habitat will be as foreign to them as a rotary telephone. We, the lawn chair gardeners, can change the world one yard at a time by limiting grass to only what we use as play space and planting the rest with beneficial, functional native, or edible plants.

Probable or Preferable Future? We Choose Our Own Future Every Day with Our Actions

Today we are, unmistakably, at a turning point in history. We are witnessing unprecedented changes on our planet with increased temperatures world-wide. In the Arctic melting polar ice caps are melting an alarming rate causing an increase in polar bear drowning because, even though polar bears are strong swimmers, they are forced to swim longer distances between ice floes. Weather patterns have become crazier, with longer periods of drought and increasingly severe storms. In Minnesota, it is suspected that moose are dying of heat stress. There are whisperings of unease as strangers make comments about global warming in passing.

Unless we change direction, we are likely to end up where we are going.

– Chinese proverb

In January 2012, the U.S. Department of Agriculture released a new Plant Hardiness Zone Map (the standard by which gardeners determine which plants are most likely to thrive at a location) that also shows a warming trend.[8] Many of us know, in our guts, that we are on the edge of something big and are witnessing climate change. It's scary, but it's also the opportune time to act

Be the change you want to see in the world.

– Mahatma Gandhi

---

8   U.S. Department of Agriculture, http://planthardiness.ars.usda.gov/PHZMWeb/ (April 2013).

and live proactively because beauty still surrounds us. The alternative is to do nothing. But imagine looking a child in the eyes in twenty years and trying to defend your apathy.

Examining Our Current Practices

A thing is right when it tends to preserve the integrity, stability, and beauty of the biotic community. It is wrong when it tends otherwise.

– Aldo Leopold

I think Aldo Leopold would call the common approach to our lawns "wrong". Below is a story I received via email that sums up how unsustainable and illogical our current lawn practices are.

Lawns and God

GOD: Francis, you know all about gardens and nature. What in the world is going on down there in the USA? What happened to the plants I started eons ago? I had a perfect, no-maintenance garden plan. Those plants grow in any type of soil, withstand drought, and multiply with abandon. The nectar from the long-lasting blossoms attracts butterflies, honey bees, and flocks of songbirds. I expected to see a vast garden of colors by now. But all I see are these green rectangles.

ST. FRANCIS: It's the tribes that settled there, Lord. The Suburbanites. They started calling your flowers "weeds" and went to great lengths to kill them and replace them with grass.

GOD: Grass? But it's so boring. It's not colorful. It doesn't attract butterflies, birds, and bees, only grubs and sod worms. It's temperamental with temperatures. Do these Suburbanites really want all that grass growing there?

ST. FRANCIS: Apparently so, Lord. They go to great pains to grow it and keep it green. They begin each spring by fertilizing grass and poisoning any other plant that crops up in the lawn.

GOD: The spring rains and warm weather probably make grass grow really fast. That must make the Suburbanites happy.

ST. FRANCIS: *Apparently not, Lord. As soon as it grows a little, they cut it, sometimes twice a week.*

GOD: *They cut it? Do they then bale it like hay?*

ST. FRANCIS: *Not exactly, Lord. Most of them rake it up and put it in bags.*

GOD: *They bag it? Why? Is it a cash crop? Do they sell it?*

ST. FRANCIS: *No, sir—just the opposite. They pay to throw it away.*

GOD: *Now, let me get this straight. They fertilize grass so it will grow. And when it does grow, they cut it off and pay to throw it away?*

ST. FRANCIS: *Yes, sir.*

GOD: *These Suburbanites must be relieved in the summer when we cut back on the rain and turn up the heat. That surely slows the growth and saves them a lot of work.*

ST. FRANCIS: *You aren't going to believe this, Lord. When the grass stops growing so fast, they drag out hoses and pay more money to water it so they can continue to mow it and pay to get rid of it.*

GOD: *What nonsense. At least they kept some of the trees. That was a sheer stroke of genius, if I do say so myself. The trees grow leaves in the spring to provide beauty and shade in the summer. In the autumn, they fall to the ground and form a natural blanket to keep moisture in the soil and protect the trees and bushes. Plus, as they rot, the leaves form compost to enhance the soil. It's a natural circle of life.*

ST. FRANCIS: *You'd better sit down, Lord. The Suburbanites have drawn a new circle. As soon as the leaves fall, they rake them into great piles and pay to have them hauled away.*

GOD: *No. What do they do to protect the shrub and tree roots in the winter and to keep the soil moist and loose?*

ST. FRANCIS: *After throwing away or composting the leaves, they go out and buy something which they call mulch. They haul it home and spread it around in place of the leaves.*

GOD: *And where do they get this mulch?*

ST. FRANCIS: *They cut down trees and grind them up to make the mulch.*

GOD: *Enough! I don't want to think about this anymore. St. Catherine, you're in charge of the arts. What movie have you scheduled for us tonight?*

ST. CATHERINE: "Dumb and Dumber," Lord. It's a real stupid movie about—

GOD: Never mind, I think I just heard the whole story from St. Francis.[9]

Using Native (Indigenous) Plants Plant Conserve Water

While maintaining some low-maintenance lawn (e.g. fine-fescue grass) as recreational space is appropriate, it is currently the most prevalent "crop" in the United States. Corn is our leading agricultural crop earning about $52 billion annually—and lawns takes up three times more space than corn![10] We have 40 million acres of lawn (62,500 square miles)[11] that provide no nutritional value to people or wildlife. .

The grasses that make up most lawns have shallow root systems and are incapable of finding their own water. In order to keep lawns green, constant watering is required; these vast expanses of green are essentially on life support. A significant amount of water in my region is used to water lawns during the summer months. For example, the City of Shoreview's Public Works Department reported that average winter water pumping is around 1.5 million gallons of water per day. During peak demand periods, mainly summer months, pumping can reach 11 million gallons a day! For the past ten years, people have been asking why water levels in area lakes have been steadily decreasing. Research by University of Minnesota students and the U.S. Geological Survey (USGS)[12] points to over-consumption of water in our region, which is depleting the Prairie du Chien-Jordan aquifers and White Bear Lake. In short, the lake sits on top of the aquifer and since the aquifer is being depleted, the lake leaks into the voided aquifer.

"Across the United States, water supplies are increasingly under pressure as populations grow. The water table has dropped hundreds of feet in many locations, and rivers and streams go dry for long stretches in various seasons . . . All along the Atlantic seaboard from

---

9   Harvey Bingham, http://www.hbingham.com/humor/godlawns.htm (April 2013).

10   Rebecca Lindsey, Looking for Lawns (study by Cristina Milesi) http://earthobservatory.nasa.gov/Features/Lawn/lawn2.php (November 8, 2005)

11   Doug Tallamy, http://bringingnaturehome.net/native-gardening/gardening-for-life (April 2013).

12   Mark Nicklawske, "USGS previews lake study findings," White Bear Press 15 February 2012 and http://mn.water.usgs.gov/about/newsletter/winter2012/ index.html

Deep rooted native prairie plants find their own water, control erosion and keep the soil from being compacted.

Florida to New York, saltwater is flowing into formerly freshwater aquifers and wells because we are pumping freshwater out faster than nature can put it back . . . **about 200 gallons of fresh, usually drinking-quality water per person per day would be required to keep up our nation's lawn surface area."[13]**

Like climate change, I would love it if someone could dismiss these aquifer findings as hooey, but no one can. Speaking of climate change, by 2050 the average temperature in central Minnesota is predicted to be five degrees Fahrenheit warmer,[14] but rain and snow fall may only increase by about two inches.[15] With increased evaporation and de-

13   Rebecca Lindsey, Looking for Lawns (study by Cristina Milesi) http://earthobservatory.nasa.gov/Features/Lawn/lawn3.php (November 8, 2005)

14   Paul Huttner, Minnesota Public Radio Climate Cast, "Climate Shock: Minnesota likely to warm another 5 degrees F by 2050," http://blogs.mprnews.org/updraft/2013/01/report_minnesota_likely_to_war/ (January 11, 2013).

15   Jeff Corney, Cedar Creek Ecosystem Science Reserve, lecture at Ramsey County Master Gardener monthly meeting, Roseville, Minnesota, April 2013.

creased precipitation, water will likely be in short supply.

To me, it is common sense to curb our unsustainable use of water. I like to garden with native plants because, once established, they are basically self-sufficient. I water them during their first growing season and then they fend for themselves. Native prairie plants can live independently because they have evolved to withstand wildfires by putting a good share of their energy into their roots. After the fires sweep through, only the tops of the plants are damaged and the plants spring right back from the long roots.

Raingardens Filter Water

In natural environments, rain soaks into the ground slowly. However, much of our landscape is now urban, full of impervious surfaces such as streets, roofs, parking lots, sidewalks, driveways, and even compacted lawns, where the water cannot soak into the ground. Many people think the dirty water on your street flushing all the crud that accumulates there gets filtered before it lands in our waters. But, nope, that is certainly not the case. Stormwater runoff, carrying pollutants such as heavy metals from brakes, salt, sand, leaves, bacteria, and grass clippings, travels into stormdrains and is piped to the nearest body of water. A pound of phosphorus, found in grass clippings, leaves, and sediment on the streets, creates about 500 pounds of algae in our waters.[16,17]

Raingardens are strategically placed gardens that intercept rain water runoff so the pollutants from streets, roofs, and parking lots don't end up in our lakes and rivers. Raingardens serve our environment by filtering out toxins from our water in the same way kidneys serve our bodies. Properly constructed raingardens will drain the water within two days so it will not become a mosquito breeding ground.

Native plants work really well in raingardens because they have long roots that keep the soil loose. Loose, non-compacted soil will continue to absorb dirty stormwater runoff long into the future. The

16   State Environmental Resource Center, http://www.serconline.org/phosphorus/fact.html (January 2005).
17   Chris Knud-Hansen, Source: Historical Perspective of the Phosphate Detergent Conflict, http://www.ecy.wa.gov/programs/wq/nonpoint/phosphorus/law.html (1994).

My Spring Raingarden

My front yard raingarden collects stormwater runoff from 17,002 square feet of impervious area (i.e. street and driveways) It also collects 12,826 square feet of runoff from my yard. The estimated total runoff my raingarden collects in a year is 181,472 gallons. In a one-inch rainfall, it will absorb 10,555 gallons from impervious areas.

<u>*Raingarden Pollutant Removal*</u>
- *Volume: 133,338 gallons/year*
- *Total Phosphorus: 0.51 pounds/year*
- *Total Solids: 240 pounds/year*

long roots of native prairie plants also serve as incredible filters. As a graduate student, I learned about "bioremediation" to clean up toxic superfund sites. In short, bioremediation is a fancy term for using biological agents, such as bacteria, fungi, or green plants—often natives—to remove or neutralize contaminants in polluted soil or water. Bacteria and fungi generally work by breaking down contaminants, such as petroleum, into less harmful substances. The plants take up a good share of the pollutants and then they are harvested and treated as the toxic waste they have become. It's almost like these native plants serve as cleverly engineered, ultra-efficient, and cheap filters.

We need to keep the streets clean—especially free of leaves and grass clippings. We also need to redirect water from our downspouts away from driveways and let raindrops soak in where they fall.

Native Critters Need Native Plants

If you think you're too small to be effective, you have never been in bed with a mosquito.

– Bette Reese

Prior to European settlement, more than 18 million acres of prairie covered Minnesota. Our prairie lands were part of the largest ecosystem in North America, which stretched from Canada to Mexico and from the Rockies to Indiana. A wealth of diverse species, habitats, and cultures thrived here. Today, less than one percent of Minnesota's native prairie remains.[18]

The biggest reason for habitat loss is population growth. The population of the United States—now more than 300 million people[19]—

---

18   Minnesota Department of Natural Resources, http://www.dnr.state.mn.us/prairierestoration/index.html (April 2013).
19   Doug Tallamy, http://bringingnaturehome.net/native-gardening/gardening-for-life (April 2013).

*Hummingbird visiting my cardinal flowers
(Lobelia cardinalis) in my raingarden.*

has doubled since I was a kid and the population continues to grow by about 8,640 people per day. Between development and agriculture, we have modified 95 percent of our lands. Anything we can do to reintroduce a little native habitat is beneficial. Of course, it's most beneficial if the space is contiguous, so you might think, "What difference will my quarter-acre make?" Well, if you get your neighbors on board and they get their neighbors on board and... Okay. You see where I am going.

A nice reward for planting a native garden is watching the birds and butterflies and knowing you're providing pollen for beneficial insects that sustain our food system. Native plants attract beautiful and diverse native butterflies, pollinators, and birds to your yard. Plants and animals evolved together over time, and have complex relationships: they depend on each other for food, habitat, and seed dispersal. For example, milkweed contains a variety of chemical compounds that make monarch caterpillars poisonous to potential predators.

Well-known professor and chair of entomology and wildlife ecology at the University of Delaware, Douglas Tallamy's research indicates that ornamentals support 29 times less biodiversity than native plants do.[20]

Invasive species, including plants, animals, and insects, have earned official standing as a leading threat—second only to habitat destruction—to native species of the United States.[21] Invasive species are non-native (or alien) to the ecosystem and are likely to cause environmental harm, economic harm, or may even harm human health.

> *"Perhaps the most extreme negative effect invasive plants have on the environment is their ability to limit biodiversity. This alters natural ecological processes by reducing the interactions of many species to the interactions of only a few. If diversity and quantity of native plants diminish, so too does the diversity and quantity of native wildlife."*[22]

Why Do We Need Biodiversity?

Biological diversity, or biodiversity, is the number and variety of organisms found within a specified geographic region. There are ethical, aesthetic, and economic reasons why we need to care about biological diversity, but there's also a fundamental reason: because the Earth's processes sustain us. Humans cannot live as the only species on this planet because other species create ecosystem services that are essential to humans. Biodiversity losses are a clear sign that our own life-support systems are failing. When biodiversity is disrupted, even if it occurs far away, the effects reverberate across the world. For example, we may experience larger hurricanes, longer droughts, crop devastation, food scarcity, and water scarcity. Conservation International's slogan is "lost there, felt here." Indeed it is.

> *"Natural ecosystems provide a wide range of benefits and "services" to people who do not have or cannot afford a local supermar-*

---

20   Doug Tallamy, http://bringingnaturehome.net/native-gardening/gardening-for-life (April 2013).
21   William Stolzenburg, Science editor, Nature Conservancy (July-August 1999).
22   Pimental et al., 2000

ket or plumbing: they supply fresh water, they filter pollutants from streams, they provide breeding ground for fisheries, they control erosion, they buffer human communities against storms and natural disasters, they harbor insects that pollinate crops or attack crop pests, they naturally take carbon dioxide out of the atmosphere."[23]

Gardening to Reduce Air Pollution and Climate Change

Another reason I tout native plants and edibles is to reduce air pollution. Did you know that running a typical gas lawn mower creates more pollution than driving a car? That seems crazy to me. At least a car gets you from point A to point B rather than just going around in circles. Reducing the amount of grass you have to mow is an easy way to improve air quality.

> *"A gasoline-powered lawn mower run for an hour puts out about the same amount of smog-forming emissions as 40 new automobiles run for an hour."*[24]

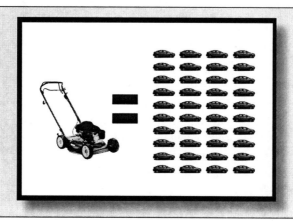

And speaking of gas, the Environmental Protection Agency estimates that more than 17 million gallons of fuel, mostly gasoline,

---

23   Thomas Friedman, *Hot, Flat and Crowded*, (New York: Farrar, Straus and Giroux, 2008), 143.
24   California Environmental Protection Agency, Air Resources Board, (May 20, 1999).

are spilled each year while refueling lawn equipment. That's more than all the oil spilled by the Exxon Valdez in the Gulf of Alaska. In addition to groundwater contamination, spilled fuel that evaporates into the air and volatile organic compounds spit out by small engines make smog-forming ozone when cooked by heat and sunlight.[25]

"Nature is like a big, complex symphony and the sun is like the bass drum. Its beat drives everything from when we had ice ages to when we had warming periods. But now the influence of humans has penetrated so deeply into this symphony that we are affecting everyday weather. It's like we are now playing really loud lead electric guitar in nature's symphony."[26]

We have found our battery electric mower to be a good option to reduce air pollution. Maybe some day we won't need as much lawn for play space and we can go back to the reel push mower we had for our small Saint Paul city lot.

Growing your own food also reduces your carbon footprint by reducing the miles your food travels. It's hard to quantify exactly, but it's intuitive that fewer emissions are produced when the following steps are eliminated: using big machinery to plant, fertilize, harvest, ship, process, package, ship again and store. In addition, consumers need to drive to the store to purchase the goods. According to Eat Low Carbon (http://www.eatlowcarbon.org) website, the food system is responsible for one-third of global greenhouse emissions. The website has a fun application where you select different foods to view their carbon emission number. With every meal you eat (and grow), you have the power to reduce climate change.

---

25   http://www.peoplepoweredmachines.com/faq-environment.htm
26   Thomas Friedman, *Hot, Flat and Crowded*, (New York: Farrar, Straus and Giroux, 2008), 113.

Gardens Better Adapted for Crazy Weather Predicted with Climate Change

I hope that I, along with 97 percent of the scientific community, are dead-wrong about climate change. I want all of these extreme weather events, instances of southern plants migrating north, and melting ice caps to be flukes. But that sure doesn't seem to be the case. Native plants (as opposed to ornamental plants) are more tolerant of extreme weather conditions such as periods of drought and excessive rain, so these plantings will be more prepared for what might be to come. Of course, all plants (yes, even lawn grass) sequester carbon dioxide to help offset emissions.

Gardens to Eliminate the Use of Chemicals

Native plants rarely need pesticides or fertilizers. If you are like me, you don't want to be putting chemicals on your food. In Chapters Six and Nine, I will talk about how you can avoid the use of chemicals through careful planning.

Evolving Ethics and Thinking about the Future

> *We abuse land because we regard it as a commodity belonging to us. When we see land as a community to which we belong, we may begin to use it with love and respect.*
>
> *– Aldo Leopold*

What will children in the future think of how we're using natural resources? As a kid learning about slavery and Nazi Germany, I remember clearly wondering how society could have gone along with these institutions and political systems that were obviously wrong. I imagine a classroom in the future where thirsty children are learning about how their drinking water was stolen from them by people who just wanted a green, ornamental yard. Perhaps they will sit in disbelief, trying to make sense of why prior generations, who knew that water is essential to sustain life, decided to use their drinking water so foolishly. Perhaps you are taken aback by my comparison of slavery and genocide to environmental degradation. Surely the impacts of environmental degradation are not as direct nor as immediate as genocide and slavery. However, by degrading the environment, we are certainly limiting the freedom of future generations. Perhaps we are even limiting their ability to survive.

As a society, we've made some progress in how we treat women, ethnic groups, and people with various sexual orientations. Not to say these issues are resolved, but there has been progress and most people recognize that all people should be treated fairly and given equal rights. It's now time to extend these same rights to the land and its critters. This is not a new concept by any means; Aldo Leopold discussed it at length in the "Land Ethic" chapter in his book, *A Sand County Almanac*, which he wrote in the 1940s. And Dr. Seuss advocated speaking for the trees in the *The Lorax* in 1971. I have hope that people will see the mutual benefits of treating the natural world with respect.

A land ethic changes the role of Homo sapiens from conqueror of the land-community to plain member and citizen of it. It implies respect for his fellow-members, and also respect for the community as such.

– Aldo Leopold, A Sand County Almanac

chapter four

Relationship Test

Snagging the Garden of Your Dreams

Exploring Different Types of Gardens

I CONFESS. Yes, I am trying to "set you up" with one of the types of gardens I am about to introduce. And, yes, the "relationship test" later in this chapter is, indeed, stacked in favor of functional gardens. My hope is that you will come to understand how great these gardens are (on the inside and out). And, at the very least, the quiz format will keep you reasonably entertained while you learn about the benefits of each type of garden.

After all of the serious information presented in the last chapter, I hope you find it motivating and inspiring to realize that by adopting one (or more) of the following gardening options, you will help bring about a lot of small changes, which, when taken as a whole, will begin to chip away at the much bigger environmental problems we are facing. Consider the following options as you begin to think about what types of gardens would work best in your yard.

The types of gardens possible are as varied as the gardeners who plant them. This may be exciting to some readers and overwhelming to others. In the next section, I will introduce four basic kinds gardens: edible, native, raingardens, and shoreline plantings. But keep in mind that it is possible to expand these garden types to include other gardening concepts.

For example, create a sensory garden using native plants and herbs. The native plants bring in beneficial insects that provide the background hum and "music" and a careful selection of colorful plants appeal to the eye. Fragrant and edible plants delight the senses of smell and taste while interesting textures treat the tactile-types.

Children's gardens are popular and I contend that absolutely any garden that is accessible to kids and free of poisonous plants could be a children's garden.

Vertical gardens that hang on houses or fences are increasingly popular as well as "square foot" or intensively planted gardens. Both of these garden types are perfect to incorporate edibles and natives.

Front yard gardens may seem to require no explanation, but the plants that typically appear in front yard gardens are changing. This part of the yard, which was once reserved for eye-catching ornamentals, has become a great place to include more edibles into your landscape. More people are transforming front lawns into gardening space. Who says you can't plant rows of lettuces along your walkway?

A Front Yard Garden in My Neighborhood

My Basic Garden Types Defined

Edible gardens typically consist of vegetables, berries, and herbs. I include native flowers in my gardens to make them "nedible" (natives + edible) gardens. Edible gardens can be planted in the ground, in raised beds, or in containers on a patio or deck. Unlike standard vegetable gardens, edible gardens are not typically planted in straight rows in a rectangular plot. Instead, the plants are worked into the landscape in an attractive way.

My Edible Garden

Native gardens are planted with indigenous, perennial plants from the area in which you live. A plant is considered native in the U.S. if it was found in the region before the area was settled by Europeans. One of the great advantages of "going native" is that these plants are well suited to the climate and soil, meaning they require less maintenance. Another important point to consider is that natives have higher quality nectar and pollen for pollinators.

A Beautiful Native Garden

Raingardens are shallow depressions planted with perennial vegetation that can handle short periods of flooding as well as drought conditions. Raingardens serve as beautiful filters to absorb stormwater runoff from streets, roofs, or driveways. The soils must drain within a day or two so they don't become a mosquito breeding ground. Raingardens should not be confused with water gardens. Water gardens are aesthetic pools or ponds often incorporating fish, waterfalls and pumps to circulate the water.

My Raingarden in Action

Shoreline stabilization plantings include using native vegetation planted along the edge of lakes or rivers. In most areas, local regulatory agencies require that shorelines be planted with native plants. Even if your area doesn't have shoreline regulations, there are at least a dozen reasons why this is beneficial to protect your water and your shore. For example, planting native vegetation along shorelines will decrease erosion, provide habitat, create beauty, and help keep water clean.

Shoreline Stabilization Planting

A Few Terms

Annuals are plants that are not hardy to your area and need to be replanted each year (or overwintered indoors).

Borders (pictured below) are gardens placed against a wall, fence, hedge, or building, with tall plants in back.

Garden bed is a garden that is viewed from all sides. Typically, the tall plants are in the middle.

Perennials are plants that come up year after year.

Raised beds are generally 2-4 feet wide, 8-feet long and 6 inches to waist high (wheel chair accessible). The frame is often made of wood (untreated lumber or cedar). A benefit to planting in raised beds is that the soil warms up faster in the spring. So, if you have a short growing season, you may be able to extend the season slightly. Also, if you have poor soils, you can avoid using the soils found on site. Another benefit is than the soil doesn't get compacted because you never need to enter the garden.

Border Garden

Relationship Test

Still wondering which type of garden is right for you? Take this quiz to discover your perfect "Lawn Chair Garden" match.

1. Sharing financial responsibilities is important.

❑ Yes   ❑ No

 If yes, you may consider…

- Edible garden with vegetables and/or herbs that cut grocery costs
- Raingardens provide tax incentives for stormwater infiltration in some counties (i.e. Hennepin in Minnesota)
- Natives save money on watering
- Shorelines planted with native plants protect soil from eroding away into the lake thereby protecting the lake and helping to maintain property values

2. It is important to me that my garden plants have a job or vocation. (They aren't just "trophy" ornamentals.)

❑ Yes   ❑ No

 If yes, you may consider…

- Edible gardens to provide food
- Raingardens to filter storm water runoff
- Native gardens to provide beauty while requiring very little maintenance
- Shorelines stabilization plantings to help maintain healthy lakes and rivers

 If you answered yes to the question above, which vocation would you find most attractive in your garden?

- Provide beauty, food, cover and habitat for wildlife (natives)
- Provide beauty and food (edible)
- Make your entrance enticing (edibles, natives)

- Fill in the challenging spot(s) in your yard, i.e. dry shady area under mature trees, wet in spring or all year, steep slope that defies mowing (natives)
- Provide a screen from your neighbors or a compost bin (natives)
- Provide a wind break or a living fence (natives)
- Extend your living space (natives, edibles)
- Provide you with materials for drying flowers and bouquets (natives)
- Keep geese out of your yard (natives, shorelines)
- Control erosion (natives)
- Help keep lakes and rivers clean by absorbing polluted runoff (raingardens and shorelines)

3. **Going out with friends and having my own social life is important to me. I do not want a controlling garden that takes over my life.**

    ❑ Yes ❑ No

    If yes, you may consider…

    - Natives
    - Raingardens
    - Shoreline stabilization garden
    - Edible gardens (Note: Edibles do require more attention at specific times of the year than other plantings on this list.)

4. **Spending quality time with in my garden is important bonding time for me and my plants.**

    ❑ Yes ❑ No

    If yes, any type of garden will work for you. If you are looking to spend a little more time with your garden, edibles are a good choice. And, if you want to spend most of your time with your garden, consider becoming a Master Gardener volunteer, working with a community garden, or gardening with kids.

5. **It is important to me that my yard/garden is low maintenance so I don't have to clean up after the plants every week.**

   ❏ Yes ❏ No

   If yes, you may consider…

   Natives. After they are established, natives only require monthly, rather than weekly, attention.

6. **It is important to me that my garden feeds my soul and strengthens my spiritual growth.**

   ❏ Yes ❏ No

   If yes, you truly are a gardener. Do what you love and feel good about.

7. **It is important to me that my garden keeps the romance going (growing) by giving me flowers.**

   ❏ Yes ❏ No

   If yes, you may conside native flowers.

8. **It is important to me that my garden is generous and charitable.**

   ❏ Yes ❏ No

   If yes, you may consider…

   Natives provide food, cover, and habitat for wildlife

   Edibles provide food for our family or food pantries

9. **Do you prefer the rough and tumble or the neat and tidy look?**

   If you prefer rough and tumble, natural and unkempt look AND you have a large area, a natural looking prairie or meadow area may be just the thing.

   If you like natural and unkempt look but you live in an urban or suburban area, the "natural look" may be just the thing to tick off your neighbors and/or get you cited for infractions on weed ordinances. Having a tidy edge such as a 2-3 foot grass border around a native planting may be all that is needed to make a native planting fit into an urban environment. Careful design, plant selection and planting in groupings are key to having native plants look tidy and manicured.

10. Have you narrowed down your preferred garden type? Are ready to seal the deal?

❑ Yes ❑ No

Remember to think about the future and how you and your garden may grow and change. Check off the following if you think you may want these things some time in the future so you can incorporate these things into a master plan.

1. ____ front yard "curb appeal"
2. ____ handle stormwater runoff
3. ____ flowers
4. ____ edibles
5. ____ a path
6. ____ less lawn/less mowing
7. ____ privacy
8. ____ a quiet place to sit in the sun or shade
9. ____ attract butterflies, birds, other wildlife
10. ____ fire pit / grill
11. ____ remedy drainage problems
12. ____ fix erosion problem
13. ____ deter geese
14. ____ pet area
15. ____ lawn for recreation
16. ____ compost bin
17. ____ other (List here)

In the next chapter, we will take a look at designs to incorporate all of the items you want in order to make sure you don't get the "seven-year itch" and wonder why your garden can't be more like your neighbor's garden.

Other Factors to Consider

Now that you have taken the test and have a few ideas about the types of garden you'd like, there are two other, very important considerations to keep in mind: the amount of sunlight your garden receives and the composition of your soil.

Does Your Yard Have a Sunny Disposition?

The amount of sunlight that shines on your yard throughout the day plays a key role in choosing your garden type. You need full sun—that means eight hours of direct sunlight—for herbs and vegetables to thrive. Partial sun is considered four to six hours of sunlight, while shade is considered less than four hours of sunlight.

Watch your yard around all sides of your house to figure out where the sun falls. Keep in mind that trees grow and will make more shade. Are your neighbor's trees shading the southern side of your yard? Does the western evening sun make it prohibitive to enjoy your deck when you want to eat outside for dinner? If you really want to have an edible garden but don't have enough sun, you may want to plant vegetables and herbs in pots placed in a wagon and move them around so they get enough sun. If you do this, be forewarned that you may be leaning towards becoming an obsessive gardener rather than a lawn chair gardener, as moving those plants around may require daily rotations.

The Importance of Structure and Fertility

Test your soil structure or texture by scooping up a handful of soil and rolling it between your fingers. If the soil feels gritty, it's a sure sign of sand. This generally means that you have good drainage, so roots will get plenty of the air they need, but you'll have to either water your plants often or plant drought-tolerant (i.e. prairie) plants. Sandy soil also means the nutrients will drain right through the soil with the water.

If your handful of soil seems sticky, or if it makes a tight ball when you squeeze it and doesn't crumble when you tap it with your finger, your soil is likely high in clay. Clay soils hold lots of moisture and nutrients, which is fine when plants are actively growing in the summer. However, during colder months, constantly moist roots are susceptible to rotting.

If your soil is between the previous descriptions, congratulations! You are the envy of all gardeners with a loamy soil. Loam is soil composed of sand, silt, and clay in relatively even concentrations and is considered ideal for gardening because it retains nutrients and water well while still allowing excess water to drain away. Most plants are very happy in this "happy medium" type of soil.

The good news is that soil is amendable. If you really want to grow a certain type of plant, find out what it needs and then engineer the soil to match. For more information about soil, see Chapter Nine.

Above: Basil (left front), Tomatoes (right front), and Perennials (back)
in My "Nedbile" (Native+Edible)
Garden Receives Full Sun

chapter five

Making Plans for a Beautiful Life Together

Designing Your Garden

A GREAT DESIGN with the right plants in the right places is, of course, the key to having a great looking garden. If you have any room in your budget, this is the point at which you may want to hire someone. I think about it this way: just because I know how to use a scissors doesn't mean I am going to cut my own hair. It is hard to do justice to garden design in a chapter or even a book since people spend years, even lifetimes, perfecting the art form of garden design. Professionals can provide a fresh perspective and offer new options that you might never think of yourself. And, it's always to your benefit to be guided by someone who is not emotionally attached to the space, someone who can be objective and bring a wealth of knowledge and tested solutions to the table.

However, for the DIYers out there who are already ignoring my advice, here is a rundown of some of the basics. If you like puzzles, you have an artistic eye, and you are willing to spend some afternoons planning, it may not be beyond your capabilities to design your own garden.

Step 1: Have Your Soil Tested

Most states have a university extension program that offers soil tests. Contact your local Master Gardener program to find out where you can have your soil tested. (There are Master Gardener programs throughout the United States and Canada.) After you locate your testing facility, follow their instructions about how to send in a sample. Be sure to take samples from all of the areas where you would like to plant. If soils were brought in or disturbed during construction, your garden soils may vary from one part of your yard to the next. You may want to get your soil tested the season before you want to plant or early in the growing season so you don't miss part of the season waiting for the results. Even though the University of Minnesota soil tests generally only take about five days to do the soil tests, this can seem like a long time if you're anxious to plant.

Step 2: Devise a Concept Plan

Drafting a concept plan of your garden may seem daunting, but it doesn't have to be. It may be helpful to start by going to an online aerial map and find your yard. Starting with a base map saves the headache of trying to draw everything to scale. You can also take a screen shot of the map and insert it into your MS Word, PowerPoint, Adobe Photoshop, or another favorite program, and print out the map from there.

On the aerial map, make sure the existing big features (such as trees and fences) show up on the map. The next step is to include the big, structural features such as trees, shrubs, and hardscapes like accent rocks or fences that you would like to add. Then, sketch in other features you may want to add, like a compost bin, swing set, etc. Look back at your wish list in Chapter Four and make sure you've included everything. Make a concept plan for your entire yard, so, as you expand your gardens over the years, all of the elements look as if they belong together. Don't worry about installing your whole plan in one year. Start small and just bite off one garden at a time. Planting in phases will help ensure that your lawn chair garden doesn't become a laborious garden.

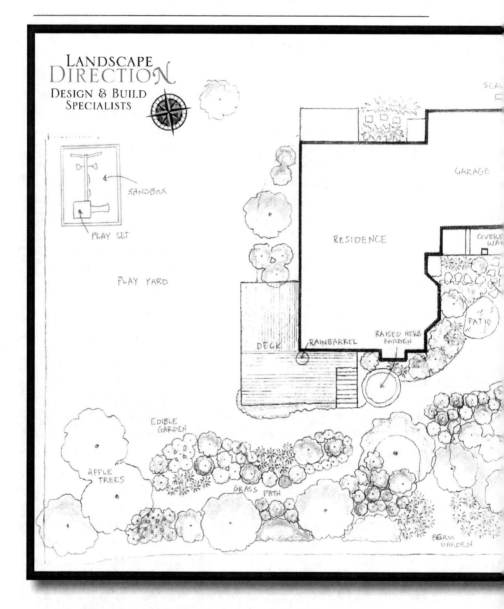

Step 3: Begin Selecting Plants

Some gardeners have a list of favorite plants they want to be sure to include already in mind. If you need some help or would like to know what is native, use an online plant finder. The Blue Thumb website (http://www.bluethumb.org/plants/) will help Midwestern garden-

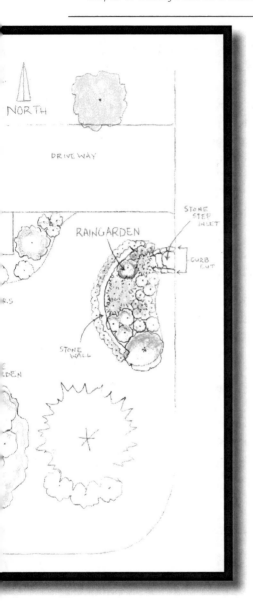

My landscape plan was created by Pete Lawrence from Landscape Direction Design & Build Specialists

On the east side, the raingarden takes street runoff.

The southern part is the perfect spot for my "nedible" (natives+edible) gardens.

The front yard patio garden is still just a concept. I haven't installed it yet.

I have installed raised beds and a cold frame in the backyard on the northern edge of our property.

ers narrow down a native plant list. If you do not live in the Midwest, search "plant finder" followed by your region and you will likely come up with a handy tool for you to use. I have searched for the perfect universal native plant finder app, but I've not yet found one. (If you know of one, let me know!) But honestly, an app cannot come close to replicating the benefits of working with a garden designer with tons of experience and an eye for aesthetics. Not yet, anyway.

The Blue Thumb—Planting for Clean Water® plant selector tool allows you to search according to sun exposure, soil moisture, color, time of bloom, and garden type. This tool includes native plants suitable for native gardens, raingardens, and shorelines, but it does not include edibles. However, herbs and vegetables generally need well-drained soil with plenty of sun, so a plant selector tool is not needed. Another nice feature of this web tool is that it searches by the common names for plants so you don't need to be an expert in Latin.

Step 4: Create a Detailed Planting Plan

If you have a large yard, consider creating separate maps for each garden. One method for planning the plantings is to make many copies of your map and do separate pages for each time of bloom. In the Midwest, your layers might be: early spring (April), late spring (May), early summer (June and July), late summer (July and August), fall (September and October), winter (November through March). Another way to create a plan is to lay old-fashioned overhead projector transparencies or tracing paper over your aerial photo map and create different layers for each bloom time. If you are computer savvy, you may want to use layers in PowerPoint, Adobe Photoshop or Illustrator and draw in the different bloom times. In addition to the bloom times, also make sure you consider plant heights, textures, and bloom colors. Next, color in the shapes with the bloom color. Finally, number each shape and include a key that provides the names of each numbered plant.

Tips

- If you are looking for a template for raingardens, you'll find plenty to choose from in the book *The Blue Thumb Guide to Raingardens*, which is available through Amazon.com or at many smaller bookstores. Go to www.BlueThumb.org/raingardens to find direct links to these bookstores.
- My "nedible" (native+edible) garden plan is available as a free

download on my website (http://www.lawnchairgardener.com/
nedibles). See Chapter Six for more information about companion
planting.

- Most plants are 2–4 feet tall. Be sure to consider plant height as
  you plan. Place the taller plants in the back of a border or in the
  middle of a bed and the shorter plants on the edges.

- Pay attention to roof overhangs—plants that grow beneath them
  won't receive adequate watering when it rains.

- When looking for plant colors, consider the color and style of
  your house. Do you have a tan house? Then plan to add some
  color to your gardens. Do you have a colonial style home with
  Ionic columns? Perhaps it would make sense to mimic the style of
  the house by planting your front entrance in a formal style with
  straight rows.

- Use the cost-calculator on http://www.bluethumb.org/raingar-
  dens to help you estimate costs.

- For maximum impact, plan on grouping a number of the same
  plant together. Single plants are likely to get lost in the landscape.
  If you have three planting areas of equal size, consider just planting two or three larger plants such as bushes, many 1–3-foot-tall
  perennials and oodles of little ground-cover type plants. (See dia-
  gram.)

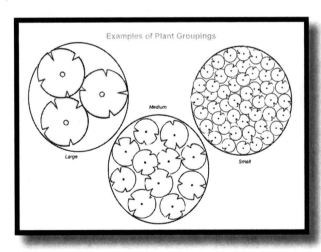

Examples of Plant Groupings

Large   Medium   Small

chapter six

The Secret to Leisurely Landscaping

Companion Planting

Companion Planting to Promote Healthy Plants

Lawn chair gardening is deeply rooted in companion planting because it greatly reduces labor and the need for chemicals. Less labor means more lawn chair time!

The key to controlling the pests is having beneficial bugs (who are naturally attracted to native plants) do the patrolling for you, keeping the slugs and thugs at bay. So how do you attract beneficial insects? Basically, just plant an array of flowers with overlapping bloom times interspersed with herbs and vegetables. This is where the "nedible" (native + edible) garden concept trumps traditional garden plots, where everything is planted in rows. Many insects are attracted to certain plants and won't bother other plants. When plants are arranged in rows, insects as well as diseases don't have to work too hard to find the next plant to attack. When edibles are planted here and there, mixed in with other types of native plants, the insects and diseases generally find the other plants to infest. There are lures that you can buy to attract beneficial insects, but why? I cannot imagine they can beat the real deals—native plants and flowering herbs. If you are looking for a specific list of plants that attract beneficial insects, try visiting http://www.pollinator.org/guides.htm. This is also available as a phone app.

Companion Planting Basics

Entire books and websites are available about companion planting. A good book is *Great Garden Companions* by Sally Jean Cunningham. While this book and others are certainly worth the read, these resources inevitably resort to lengthy lists of companion planting pairs long enough to make a person's eyes cross. What's more, I have found a lot of conflicting information on these lists, because companion planting is as much of an art as it is a science. Since I find these lists intimidating and unapproachable, I am assuming others might too so I have simplified companion planting to three basic concepts.

Concept 1: Meet The "Covergirls": Easy, Breezy and Beautiful

If vegetables, herbs and flowers are planted in proximity to each other, pest problems will likely be reduced. A general rule of thumb is to plant a vegetable with a fragrant herb (to confuse pests with the strong scent) and/or a flower to attract beneficial pollinators, which eat the bad bugs.

The Covergirl "Easy, Breezy, Beautiful" slogan might serve as a silly tool to remember this concept. "Easy" stands for "Easy Peas-y" and refers to peas and other edibles that we are trying to protect from pests. Next, "Breezy" refers to herbs because they are fragrant in the breeze. Dill, rosemary and basil are very commonly used herbs. It is thought that the fragrance of herbs helps deter insect pests by disorienting them. Finally, "Beautiful" refers to attractive flowering plants that provide nectar, pollen, and habitat for beneficial insects. Flowers in the "Aster family" (Asteraceae) or "Sunflower family" (Compositae) are generally considered good companions. Since these are two of the largest plant families in the world, most any flower chosen will be a good choice.

Concept 2: Finding a Partner—Opposites Attract

Much like people, opposite plants attract. (But, unlike people, they most likely won't spend the rest of their lives driving each other crazy.) Plant sun-loving plants with shade-loving ones so the sun-loving plants can offer shade to their companions (e.g, Maximilian sunflower with lettuce). Plant deeply rooted plants with shallowly rooted plants (e.g. sweet potatoes with lettuces). Plant short plants with tall (e.g, carrots and corn), and fast growing with slow growing (radishes with broccoli). Early bloomers work well with late bloomers (chives with asters), and plant "heavy-feeders" (requiring nutrient-rich soil) with "light-feeders" such as onions.

How do you know which plants are heavy-feeders? Not surprisingly, larger plants such cucumbers, squash, pumpkins, corn, and tomatoes are typically heavier feeders. An exception is that peppers and celery are not particularly large, but also need fertile soil. Moderate feeders include many mid-sized plants like broccoli, Brussels sprouts, cabbage, cauliflower, kale, greens, and parsley. Light feeders include smaller plants like beets, carrots, garlic, leeks, onions, potatoes, radishes, and turnips.

Beans, peas, and clover help build soil. With the help of bacteria in the ground, they excrete atmospheric nitrogen for their own use and for any neighboring plants.

Concept 3: Traveling the World

In ecology, plants live in "communities." In *Great Garden Companions*, Cunningham groups companion plants into "neighborhoods." Her approach is a clever way to get one's arms around lengthy lists of compatible companion plants. However, I still found the information hard to remember because the plants within her "neighborhoods" didn't have any obvious association. After studying her neighborhoods for some time, I connected the types of foods that make up that her "neighborhoods" with popular cuisines from around the world. So, I adapted Cunningham's "neighborhoods" to be my gardening beds as well, but I call the beds "countries" (see charts on pages 58-65).

When considering tomatoes and basil, who doesn't think of Italian cooking? This is how Cunningham's tomato neighborhood became my "Italy." And if a person were to play a word association game using the word "potato," the country of "Ireland" might be a popular guess. As a result, the neighborhood containing potatoes, peas and rosemary has become my "Ireland." Now, let's hop on over to France. A flavor base used in a wide variety of French dishes, *mirepoix*, consists of carrots, onions and celery, so I call Sally's carrots, onions, and greens neighborhood "France." (Never mind that Sally doesn't specifically list celery. Celery and carrots are in the same botanical family.)

My "Germany" consists largely of plants in the cabbage family because, of course, traditional German sauerkraut starts out as cabbage. Since my family actually doesn't eat a lot of cabbage, I plant other vegetables that have "heads" like broccoli and cauliflower. And perhaps surprisingly, radishes, kale, and Swiss chard also belong to the cabbage family.

The Iroquois are known for the "Three Sisters" garden of corn, beans and squash so that section is my "North American" area. (Since the Iroquois span present day United States and Canada, I did not feel right about just giving it a single country name.)

My last country, "Greece," is where my perennial plants reside. Why? Because perennial plants live for a long time and so do the people on the isolated Greek island of Ikaria. In fact, this island is home to more healthy people over 90 than any other place on the planet.

It is important to rotate garden beds to help manage soil fertility and also to help avoid or reduce problems with soil-borne diseases and some soil-dwelling insects to prevent diseases from spreading.

Companion Planting Basics

Opposites Attract

Meet the "Covergirls"   Traveling the World

The above three-legged stool demonstrates
three basic companion planting concepts.

1. **Meet the "Covergirls"**—Easy-Peasy, Breezy and Beautiful. Vegetables planted with a fragrant herb (to confuse pests with strong scent) and/or a flower to bring in beneficial pollinators to eat the bad bugs is beneficial.

2. **Opposites Attract**—A general rule of thumb is to have plants with opposites growing needs planted together.

3. **Traveling the World**—Edibles in garden beds can be grouped by ethnic cuisines.

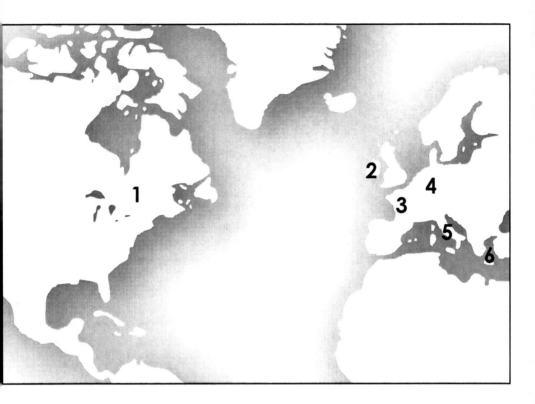

A World Tour Right at Home

The "countries" are listed on the table (on the following pages) and on the map in geographic proximity to one another—for people like me who need a "visual map!"

This table (except the first column) is adapted from <u>Great Garden Companions</u>, by Sally Jean Cunningham, Master Gardener, Cornell Cooperative Extension, p. 46-47

Companion Planting by Countries, Cuisines, Families & Ambassadors

Continents/ Countries	Cuisine	Family	Ambassadors *(Italics indicates non-native, non-herb; not "Lawn Chair" style)*
1. North America	Corn, Beans & Squash	Squash family, corn, pole beans	Dill, sturdy flowers in Aster family that act as a trellis such as sunflowers, *borage, nasturtiums*
2. Ireland	Potatoes	Potatoes, beans, peas	Dill, rosemary, Aster family flowers such as *Calendulas, cosmos, sweet Annie, ~~daisies~~ (Can be invasive!)*
3. France *(mirepoix is a bed of diced braising vegetables-carrots, celery, onions*	Roots and Greens	Carrots, greens, onions	Dill, fennel, short Aster family flowers, caraway, chamomile, *cleome, dwarf cosmos, Queen-Anne's-lace, Iceland poppies*
4. Germany	Cabbage, broccoli, cauliflower, kale	Cabbage family, lettuce, root crops	Asters, rosemary, sage, thyme, chamomile, *calendulas, chrysanthemums, cosmos, marigolds*

Please note!

The plants listed on the table in italics denote that they are not "Lawn Chair" style-meaning either that they are not native and/or not a common kitchen herb. The plants that have a line through them may be invasive. Even though they are recommend by Cunningham, I do not recommend them because they are listed as a noxious weed by the Minnesota Department of Natural Resources. (Yes, sadly, lovely oxeye daises are an invasive plant needing control.)

Rotation *(I rotate all beds every other year to keep them on same timeline)*	Notes
every 3 years	This trio is a traditional Native American combination. Beans will climb corn. Plant vine crops and nasturtiums in hills or 3-ft. wide sections among corn. If you don't grow corn, use stakes, teepees trellises to support beans
at least every 3 years	Plant potatoes in rows with room for hilling. Plant beans or peas in wide rows. Use potatoes to break in new garden areas. All the trenching and digging really works the soil and helps reduce weeds.
rotate carrots every 2 years. Lettuce doesn't need to be rotated	Interplant greens, carrots and onions. Or, plant them in blocks side by side. Use thinnings in salads. After harvesting lettuce, plant kale or fall greens.
at least every 2-3 years	Plant crops in 2-1-2 or 3-2-3 patterns with groundcover in between, or tuck onions, carrots or beets around the crops. Lettuce grows well in the shade of broccoli leaves. Cover all crops with row covers from planting until harvest.

Companion Planting by Countries, Cuisines, Families & Ambassadors

Continents/ Countries	Cuisine	Family	Ambassadors (Italics indicates non-native, non-herb; not "Lawn Chair" style)
5. Italian	Tomatoes and Basil	Tomatoes, peppers, eggplant, (greens)	Basil, parsley, any tall Aster Family flower, *cleome, cosmos, Queen Anne's Lace*
6. Greek Island of Ikaria (which is known for lon-gevity)	Perennial Crop	Asparagus, horseradish, strawberries, rhubarb, raspberries	Chives, asters, bee balm, black-eyed Susans, creeping thyme, yarrow (for horseradish), dill, chamomile, *sweet alyssum, hollyhocks, sweet Annie* (for asparagus), *cosmos, lovage, sunflowers, borage, nastur-tiums, ~~tansy, daisies~~ (Invasives!)*

Rotation *(I rotate all beds every other year to keep them on same timeline)*	Notes
every 4 years	Early in the season, plant greens around edge. By the time the tomatoes grow large, the greens will be harvested.
3 year rotation	Aggressive spreader like horseradish paired with bee balm. Hollyhocks, cosmos sparingly in asparagus patch.

Irish

Native American

French

Above Arrows Indicate Crop Rotation

It is important to rotate garden beds to help manage soil fertility and also to help avoid or reduce problems with soilborne diseases and some soil-dwelling insects to prevent diseases from spreading.

Plan Drawing by Jodi Refsland

Download My Planting Plans

Please visit the "Nedibles" (Natives+Edibles) page on my website to download my planting plans.

http://www.lawnchairgardener.com/nedibles

chapter seven

Start Your Own or Adopt?

Starting Plants by Seed or Buying Plants

Winter Seed Sowing

If you spent a lot of your budget hiring a designer, starting seeds in the winter is a fantastic way to save on plant costs. You can start hundreds of plants for under $20. It's also fun to get your hands dirty and plant in the winter. Plus, if you use this method of starting seeds, you don't have to dedicate valuable indoor living space to flats of plants or invest in bulky grow lights that are on all night, making your neighbors raise their eyebrows at the thought of what you may be growing in there. Believe me, I have started seeds indoors before and setting up such an elaborate operation can make you feel a little self-conscious. Once I even considered hanging a sign in the front window stating "I'm a Master Gardener. I am just growing kitchen herbs—nothing illegal!"

What is winter sowing? One method involves planting seeds in milk jugs (or other containers) and setting the jugs outside until spring. The milk jugs serve as mini-greenhouses. The seeds don't do much until the weather gets warmer, but they definitely get a jump-start on the season and start growing a good month or two before you could get them planted in the ground. If you have a short growing season, this is a big deal.

Winter and Spring Sowing Instructions

For those in the zone 4 (near Minneapolis/St. Paul, Minnesota), follow this schedule when sowing seeds in winter and spring. Plant perennials (such as native plants that come back year after year) in January, February, or March. Plant herbs and vegetables anytime between April 1 and April 20. Anytime after late April, set the jugs aside and plant seeds directly into the ground. For other zones, plant perennials during your coldest months and plant herbs and vegetables 6-8 weeks before you'd expect to be able to plant in the ground.

Supplies Needed

- Empty milk jugs (Do you need a bunch in a hurry? Ask your local coffee shop(s) to save them for you. If you're going to store them for a while before you use them, make sure they are well rinsed with no caps so you don't have to deal with the unpleasant odor of spoiled milk. You can use other kinds of clamshell-type plastic containers, but I've found that milk jugs are pretty easy to acquire.)
- Utility knife
- Potting soil
- Seeds
- Watering can or pitcher
- Large storage containers or laundry tub
- Garden marker (a special marker usually sold at garden stores that doesn't fade like permanent markers do)
- Plant labels (popsicle sticks or store-bought labels)
- Duct tape. Clear is the best, but white is all right too.

1. Use a utility knife to cut four 1-inch slits in the bottom of each milk jug. Twist the knife to make the slits into holes (picture 1).

2. About 5 inches from bottom of each milk jug, use the utility knife to cut around the jug horizontally from one side of the handle to the other horizontally (picture 2). Be sure to leave about one inch of the jug uncut. This piece will act as a hinge for opening and closing the jugs.

3. Grab the handle and pull it back to open the jug. It may be helpful to put a weight in the top half of the jug to keep it out of your way when you're adding the soil and seeds. A rock will do the trick.

4. Add soil to the jug, filling it to a level about 1–2 inches below cut line (picture 3).

5. Place the jug in the utility tub. Water the soil until it is muddy and you see water coming out of the bottom.

6. Flatten the soil so there aren't any peaks or valleys.

7. Add as many seeds as you wish.

9. Cover the seeds with soil as instructed on the seed packet. As a rule of thumb, a seed should be sown at a depth equal to its longest side. If seeds are very tiny, it's not necessary to cover with soil.

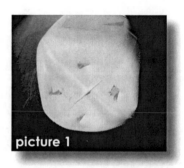

picture 1

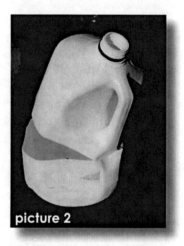

picture 2

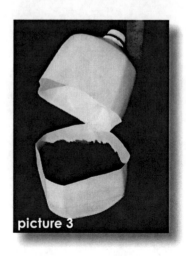

picture 3

picture 4

10. Lightly add more water to moisten.

11. Add a plant label inside the container with the name of plant, color, light requirements, and height. This label will go into the garden. (You can do this step later, but it's nice to do it when you have the seed packet handy.)

12. Close the cover and duct tape the jug back together. Clear or white duct tape is best because darker colors get hot and gooey in the heat of the sun, making it hard to remove the tape in the spring without shaking up the plant (picture 4).

13. Label the outside of the jug with the plant name and date.

14. Place the jugs outside on the east, south, or west side of your house (anywhere but the north side, where it likely won't get enough sun). You can put containers on patios, in gardens, on grass, on picnic tables, or on decks. Do not place them under decks, awnings, or roof lines because they won't get any rain. It's fine if the snow piles up on top of the containers. Just make sure there's no cap on the jug—precipitation will keep the soil moist.

For bakery, takeout, produce, or rotisserie chicken containers, follow the same instructions as for the milk jugs with the following exceptions.

- Add holes in top of the container.
- Add as much soil as you can.
- Place plant label on its side inside the container.
- There's no need to tape the container unless it won't stay closed.

Additional Notes:

Watch containers for drying and, if necessary, water with the hose attachment on mist. As the weather warms up, you may need to open the containers during the day so the seedlings don't overheat, and close the containers at night if temperatures are too cool or below freezing. On hot spring days, you might want to move your containers to the east side of your home to receive less sun so they don't completely dry out.

You can cut off the lid entirely when the weather warms up and it is past the risk of frost. (Around mid-May for zone 4.) Wait for mature roots before dividing and planting. To test if the roots are mature, gently tip the jug onto your open palm. If the soil holds together pretty well, the roots are probably mature.

Do the above instructions sound like a pain? Or, did you miss your window because you're reading this in May? No worries. Just buy plants! For tips about purchasing plants, keep reading.

Where Should I Get My Plants?

Buying from small, local nurseries might be the easiest way to ensure you're getting truly native plants that aren't laced with harmful pesticides. To find local nurseries that sell natives in the Midwest, check out http://www.bluethumb.org. Nationwide, http://www.plantnative.org has a great list of native plant nurseries. Farmers' markets or Master Gardener plant sales may be good options too. I avoid buying perennials from big box stores because their plants are most likely not truly native or grown with local seed. Therefore, they may not be hardy (survive the winter). Even though a big box store plant might be called "Black-eyed Susan" or something native to your area, many species are known to occur across wide ranges of geography, climate, and environmental conditions. Sub-groups of these species have become adapted to various local conditions within these wider ranges. These are called "local ecotypes". You will want to use the best-adapted plants for a landscape project. Local ecotype native plants are clearly well adapted to local conditions. This means plant seed should come from plants grown no farther than 200 miles (300 miles for trees and shrubs) from the garden where they will be planted. If the nursery where you are purchasing plants doesn't know where the seeds are from, you may want to shop elsewhere.

What's the difference between a native plant and a "cultivar"?

A cultivar (short for "cultivated" and "variety") isn't grown by Mother Nature—it's developed by humans for unique colors, variegated foliage, or double flowers. Cultivars keep their characteristics (bloom color, size, light preferences, etc.) only when reproduced by plant breeders. If left to their own devices, cultivated plants can revert back to their original characteristics. Most turf grasses as well as annual and perennial bedding plants are cultivars. There are cultivars that have been selected and bred from species native to the United States too.

Although these cultivars are often showier or better "behaved"—for example, they may be bred to not get so tall and lanky—their genetic make-up is considered to be somewhat narrowed and altered from the original source material. They also generally contain less pollen and nectar and do not provide quality nutrition for wildlife and pollinators. Sometimes the cultivar blooms are a different shape and pollinators cannot even enter the bloom. In general, cultivars are not as beneficial to ecosystems.

How Can You Tell if You're Buying a Cultivar?

On the plant tag, the cultivar name is capitalized and written in single quotes, as in New England Aster 'Purple Dome.' A cultivar may also be designated by the letters "cv" before the name with no quotes. A hybrid is a cross between two different species of the same genus. Hybrids can occur in the wild or in cultivation. Hybrids are denoted with an "x" after the Latin name on plant tags.

Please note that if you are planting a shoreline stabilization project, environmental regulations state that you must use only local ecotype native plants. Regardless of their origin, cultivars and non-native plants should not be introduced to the shoreland because they may invade existing native plant communities, their root systems may not adequately protect the shoreline from erosion, and they may not provide shelter and food for native animals. It's very difficult for Departments of Natural Resources and other local units of government such as watershed districts to enforce these regulations; therefore it is up to residents to plant responsibly.

Beware of getting "free" plants—especially if your pal doesn't know the name of it and/or the origin of the plant. This is one of the many sneaky methods of how invasive plants become invasive.

Let's Talk about the Birds and the Bees— and their Declining Populations

Perhaps it is not appropriate for me to discuss the "birds and the bees," but we all know that this is a pivotal topic. Birds, bees and other pollinating insects' "deeds" of transferring pollen from the male flower parts to the female flower parts of a flower resulting in fertilization and the production of seeds is an invaluable service. Think about the labor costs if we had to pay workers to do this to produce our fruits and vegetables. Most of us wouldn't even know quite what to do. (How awkward.) It's true that some crops are pollinated by birds, bats and even wind, but most rely on pollinating insects—especially bees. The problem is, pollinators are in peril with a few huge strikes against them.

According to Marla Spivak, a bee researcher at the University of Minnesota, managed bee colonies are experiencing unsustainable annual losses around 30 percent of their population since the winter of 2006-2007. Native bee populations are harder to track, but are also in decline.

Problems with Pesticides

Habitat loss combined with a "wonder" class of insecticides, neonicotinoids, that was introduced by Bayer in mid 1990s are making survival for our insect friends a challenge. This chemical is related to nicotine and attacks the insects' nervous systems. Neonicotinoids, also called neonics, are systemic, meaning they permeate the whole plant, including the nectar and pollen and they persist for years unlike other insecticides. The neonicotinoids do not kill the insects on contact, but impair the insects' abilities to navigate back to their hives or nests. In addition, insects, like bees, feed on the nectar and bring pollen back to their brood slowly weakening the whole colony with these neuro-toxins making them more susceptible to disease. This explains why so many bees are dying of viruses.

Neonics are often applied to seeds like corn. In fact, virtually the entire U.S. corn crop uses treated seeds which makes up a very large land mass. However, it's not just the large-scale farmers we need to point our fingers at. The concentration of these insecticides is actually higher in urban landscape than in agricultural fields.

> *"While the sheer scale of corn production probably makes it the most common way bees are exposed to imidacloprid and other neonics, garden, landscape, and nursery uses can't be discounted as a factor in declining bee health. In fact, according to Vera Krischik, an entomologist at the University of Minnesota, imidacloprid expresses itself in soil-treated plants like garden flowers at a much higher dose than it does for seed-treated plants like corn. In her research, she found that imidacloprid in nectar from seed-treated plants tend to hover at less than 1 part per billion, while soil-treated plants produced nectar that*

contains as much as 40 parts per billion."[27]

In the landscape realm, many products that offer broad-spectrum pest control (i.e., it kills a wide range of insects) and synthetic fertilizer in one convenient product contain imidacloprid, a common type of neonicotinoid. These products are often sprinkled on the soil and are taken up by the plants' roots and spread through the entire plant. Neonics are commonly used in potting soil by growers so well-meaning consumers seeking "bee-friendly" plants may be inadvertently doing more harm than good. If the retailers are not growing their own plants, they may not even realize the chemical was applied in the growing process since current plant labelling laws do not require disclosure of chemicals.

Other chemicals in the neonicotinoid class include acetamiprid, clothianidin, imidacloprid, nitenpyram, nithiazine, sulfoxaflor, thiacloprid and thiamethoxam. My philosophy is to avoid all chemicals I cannot pronounce and buy my plants from a trusted source so I know I am not accidentally harming my insect friends.

Taking Insects Under Our Wings

The European Union has restricted the use of neonicotinoids due to evidence of a connection to honey bee colony collapse disorder, but, so far, the U.S. hasn't followed suit despite the lawsuits against the Environmental Protection Agency by U.S. beekeepers and sustainable agriculture advocates accusing the agency of inadequate toxicity evaluations and allowing registration of the pesticides to stand on insufficient industry studies.

Where does this information leave the consumer? The simplest form of action is voting with our dollars and demanding transparency about seeds, plants and products from retailers. Before purchasing any seeds, be sure to understand how the seeds were collected and whether the seed was treated.

---

27   http://www.motherjones.com/tom-philpott/2012/01/bee-killing-pesticides-not-just-corn-fields

chapter eight

Let's Get the Party Started!

Tools on the Invitation List

What to Wear

Slip-on garden shoes, gardening gloves, a hat, long-sleeved, light-colored shirt and long pants—yes, there's a reason why gardeners have sort of a gardening uniform. I used to puzzle about why hard-core gardeners dressed like they were taking a safari. But after a bug bite on my leg became infected from scratching it with dirty finger nails and the redness surrounding it was the size of a dinner plate, I came to realize how much sense it makes to wear protective clothing. It's also nice to not mess around with sunscreen and bug spray that needs to be showered off after a short stint in the garden. Just slip out of your clothes and leave the dirt hanging in the entry or in the garage. It really saves on laundry to just wear the same long-sleeved, quick-dry shirt and pants over and over. My gardening clothes need to be practically standing up on their own before I deem them ready to be washed.

Most people do not want to invite "tools" to their parties, but here's my favorite guest list.

Who's Invited

A.   Garden gloves

B.   Hand spade or gardening knife for planting small plants. (Hand rakes generally come as a set with hand spades, but I rarely use my hand rake.)

C.   Garden markers for labeling plants. Really, they are called "Garden markers" and they last a LOT longer than a so-called permanent marker that won't make it through even one Minnesota winter.

D.   Plant labels. There are so many to choose from—fancy metal ones, basic plastic ones, tongue depressors. I say buy what you like or can afford. I have even used plastic silverware when I was in a pinch and didn't feel like running out to get different ones. But remember to map out and/or take a picture so you have a hard copy in the house, because no marker is permanent. Kids, storms, animals—who knows? They just disappear!

E.   Shears for trimming perennials and bushes

F.   Pruner for cutting small, woody branches

G.   Sprinklers and/or soaker hoses. Soaker hoses conserve water, are typically left in place for the season and need to be pretty close to the plants. Sprinklers, on the other hand, can be moved more easily and water a larger area.

H.   Timers to attach to hoses to automate watering

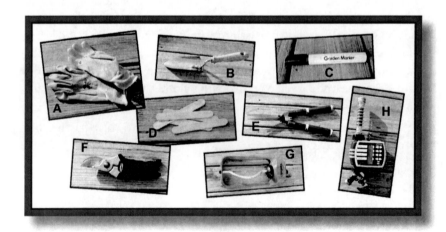

(I-P are pictured from left to right)

I.   Pitch fork if you have any amount of wood chips or straw mulch to move around

J.   Rounded shovel (I like long-handled ones so I have more leverage to dig up plants with stubborn roots.)

K.   Metal leaf rake (not a plastic leaf rake or a garden rake) because it is gentler and it doesn't pull the plants completely out of the ground when you are raking up the trimmings and leaves.

L.   Square shovel if you have any sod to remove

M.   String trimmer if you have a big perennial bed (otherwise a shears is sufficient)

N.   A tarp is helpful to rake debris onto. If you have a smaller garden, tarp bags (pictured next to wheelbarrow) work better than plastic garbage bags because they have wider opening, stand open on their own and can be reused for years.

O.   Hoses (consider buying ones that are BPA-free/phthalate-free)

P.   Wheelbarrow—I found out they make fold-up wheelbarrows after I already bought mine. This seems like a handy option if you have limited garage space like I do.

My all time favorite tool, however, is a gardening knife (pictured above). It is very versatile because it can be used for digging, weeding, scoring root balls, and dividing.

When I go out for a gardening session, I pretty much haul all of my tools out with me in a wheelbarrow (a big pail could work too). Why? Otherwise I end up walking back and forth between the garage and the garden constantly, which is more exercise than I'm usually looking for. If I don't bring everything out, I go out to pull a few weeds, but then I realize I need a container to put the weeds into. Next, I realize I need a little garbage container for the garbage that "grows" in the compost since every time it rains little bits of trash emerge from the compost that came from the county compost site. Then I realize that something needs to be staked or that the squirrels dug up a plant and it needs to be replanted...

I organize my wheelbarrow like this: a container (old pot from something recently planted or an ice cream bucket) for small hand tools and gloves, a container for weeds, a container for garbage, and a container for soil. I like to have a container of soil because it's amazing how often you have just a little too much or too little dirt when you're planting.

chapter nine

Getting Down to Earth

Preparing the Soil and Planting

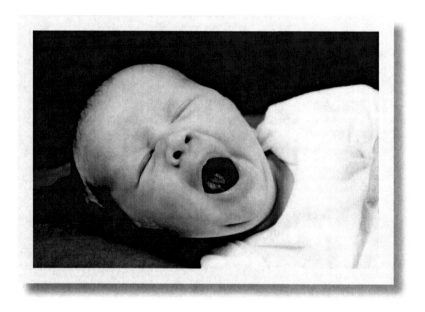

ARE YOU STIFLING A YAWN RIGHT NOW? You want to skip this section on soil, don't you? Good news! If you're planting natives that are well suited for their sites, you can go straight to the planting section! However, if you're planting herbs and vegetables, it's imperative that you get your soil right. I know it's tempting to want to move right to the fun, actionable part of planting, but preparing soil is a little like get-

There are 900 billion microorganisms in a pound of soil. As a teacher, I've found that once gardeners realize that soil is alive, they treat it with a lot more respect.

–Sally Cunningham, Great Garden Companions, p. 23

ting ready to paint. If you don't put down a drop cloth, you'll wish you had made the effort. Once plants are in, it will be very difficult to amend the soil. Good soil preparation saves you from trouble later because you'll have healthier plants that will be better able to withstand disease or pests.

Once you've gotten your soil test back, you may learn that it needs amendments. A trip to your local garden center might leave you baffled by the multitude of products available. Here's a brief rundown.

Compost: The rich, black soil-like result of decomposed leaves and other plant materials. Compost is high in organic matter content and is the perfect plant food, soil amendment, and disease fighter. You want "finished compost," where few to none of the original ingredients are discernible. A couple of twigs here and there are fine, but lots of wood chips are not. "Leaf compost" should look like compost, not leaves. I make my own compost, but when I was establishing large gardens that required more compost than I had, I got compost from the county compost site for free. Maybe your county offers it too.

Soil: The basic term for what's already there, a.k.a. your "dirt". Most un-amended soils contain a lot of sand or clay, and their organic matter content is generally very low. A bag in the store that says "garden soil" tells you nothing about how much organic matter it contains. I would recommend only buying clearly labeled products or ask to open up a bag and roll it between your fingers so you can get an idea of what the soil is like.

Humus: Latin for "soil," this generally refers to components of soil that are rich in organic matter, whether from added compost or from the natural decomposition of plant material that occurs on forest floors. In retail, humus is an incredibly slippery term that may refer to compost, harvested forest soil, or to nothing at all. "Rich in humus" means the material contains some organic matter, but maybe a lot of inert filler too. Completely finished compost made from mixed yard waste is virtually 100 percent humus.

Topsoil: Technically, this refers to the uppermost 6 to 12 inches of a soil or "the top of the soil." In the woods, this would be the most humus-rich portion. In commerce, it is a virtually meaningless term. It is not compost in any way. If you really want "topsoil," that is, the most humus-rich portion of a harvested soil, look for material that's dark in color. Screened topsoil is better than unscreened because the rocks will have been removed and the particles will be smaller, which is good.

Composted soil: Although this term is thrown around quite a bit, it is a misnomer. Soil is already "done" and cannot be composted. If someone offers you "composted soil," ask if they meant to say compost or topsoil. Be very wary about any further advice they impart.

Compost tea: Compost teas are mixtures made by putting compost (or sometimes manure) in a bucket of water with sugar or molasses to produce a "tea." Sometimes aeration is used in this process too. The theory is that good bacteria will flourish and outmaneuver the bad bacteria to fight disease. In reality, there is no proof that this tea works. I am a little embarrassed to admit that I was enticed by this seemingly silver bullet so my husband and I tried it a few years ago. We saw no difference where we applied it. Even University of Minnesota researchers were unable to get positive results. This leads me to believe that the average gardener won't have more success with their home brews made in their sheds. Moreover, there is a body of research indicating that Escherichia coli (a.k.a E. coli) and salmonella thrive in these conditions.[28] Scary! For that reason alone, I am wary of this method.

---

28   Jeff Gillman, *The Truth About Organic Gardening*, (Portland: Timber Press, 2008), 127-128.

Bio-solids: Compost-like product made from the sludge (human waste) at water treatment plants. Bio-solids are controversial because traces of antibiotics and other pharmaceutical medications show up in these "bio-solid" composts. I wouldn't use it.

Composted manure: The rich, black soil-like result of decomposed animal waste and their bedding. Completely composted manure (also called "aged" or "well rotted") looks like compost, but is not compost per se. Composted manures are very high in organic matter, but may be too nitrogen rich to use alone on flowering plants. This is especially true of horse and poultry manures, which often grow enormous plants with few fruits and flowers. Composted manures are best used as specific fertilizers, not as a basic soil amendment. Raw manure should never be used. If you have access to raw barnyard manure, just mix it into a "regular" compost pile, where it will enhance the finished product. Or, pile it up and allow it to compost on its own.

Ah, Compost!

Why do gardeners get all googly-eyed about good compost? Compost is the gold standard of soil amendments and is quite magical. It drains well, it is super nutrient rich, it helps control erosion, and it eliminates the need for fertilizers and possibly even pesticides. Also, it is safe to use because composting kills pathogenic organisms like E. coli and salmonella. However, you can have too much compost causing mineral toxicities so be sure to apply in accordance with your soil test results. A general rule is to apply a layer 1/3 to 1/2 inch deep every other year.[29] I just spread the compost on top and work it in as I plant. I follow a permaculture school of thought of disturbing the soil as little as possible to keep the nemotodes and othe wonder organisms in tact. Plus, it's less work than tilling it in. (And I stand by my name of being a lawn chair gardener.)

Be sure you know the source of the compost you're using. If you are getting it from a county compost site, most likely the source is yard waste like leaves and grass clippings where there is no significant

---

29   Jeff Gillman, *The Truth About Organic Gardening*, (Portland: Timber Press, 2008), 30.

source for heavy metal pollutants. Most likely these facilities test every four months for agricultural suitability: pH, salts, electrical conductivity (how available nutrients are), carbon/nitrogen ratio, sodium and all of the major and minor fertility elements, such as nitrogen, phosphorus, potassium, sulfur, copper, molybdenum, zinc, calcium, manganese, magnesium, and boron, etc.

Composting at Home

I really encourage you to find a sunny location for your compost bin and compost at home. It's really simple to do and you'll have the added benefit of knowing you will have safe compost. If you have any children in your life, it's also a great way to teach about recycling and life cycles. If you have a yard with a lot of trees, it gets pretty tough to be able to compost all of your own leaves, but it's easy to at least manage your own vegetable and fruit scraps. You might be surprised by how much less garbage you produce when you compost your fruit and vegetable scraps. You can bring the material you cannot compost at home to a county compost site. Some waste haulers even do curbside bins. I love not having to haul my compost away on a Saturday morning when I'd rather be going out for a bike ride.

Directions for Composting

1. Just add "green" material like fruit and vegetable scraps and/ or grass clippings. (However, it's best to just leave grass clippings on your grass because it acts like fertilizer). Be careful not to add any animal products like egg shells or meat scraps, because they might attract vermin to your bin.
2. If the bin gets stinky, add "brown" materials like dried leaves or brown paper bags. Consider keeping a bag of leaves from the previous fall so you have it to add to your compost in July.
3. Keep it moist and stir it occasionally and let the microscopic organisms work their magic.
4. In a season or two, you'll have finished compost. Some people like to have two bins so they can have a finishing bin and a fresh scraps bin.

I've tried two different types of commercial bins and I prefer the stationary type with a little door that slides up on the bottom (pictured left) so you can shovel out the finished compost. I also tried the tumbler type that is set on a stand so it can be flipped it over from time to time (pictured right). The trouble with the tumbler bin is the finished material keeps mixing with the unfinished compost so it's tough to remove the finished compost a little at a time. You have to wait until the whole bin is finished.

Soil pH

Soil pH can be determined by sending a sample of the soil to a soil testing facility. Again, many universities have testing facilities. The University of Minnesota has detailed instructions at this link: http://soiltest.cfans.umn.edu

Most things that you would like to grow will most likely do just fine with your soil's pH (level of acidity or alkalinity). However, if you are planning to grow blueberries, they require acidic, well-drained soils, which are not common in most Minnesota landscape situations.

Establishing Blueberries

Blueberries are great plants to have in your yard because they are beautiful all year round and provide healthy and delicious fruit. Blueberry plants grow best in a sunny location with acid soils (pH 4.0 to 5.0) that are well-drained, loose, and high in organic matter.

Blueberry plants are long-lived (30 to 50 years or perhaps even longer), so considerable time and effort in preparing the planting site is wise. Soils not within the range of pH acceptability for blueberry plant growth must be prepared before planting. If the pH is too high, the growth of the plant is slowed and the leaves turn yellow. If the pH is too high for an extended period of time, the plants will die. When several plants are to be grown together, you'll have better results to amend the entire bed rather than amending holes for individual plants.

There are many "recipes" on how to amend soil for blueberries. The simplest I've seen is University of Minnesota Extension Education, Karl Foord's formula listed below. For more information, check out http://blog.lib.umn.edu/efans/ygnews/2011/04/creating-a-soil-mix-for-bluebe.html.

Blueberry Soil Mix:

50% Sphagnum peat moss (pH of 3.6 to 4.2)

10% Original soil (pH 7 clay loam)

10% Compost (likely pH at 7)

10% Sand Inexpensive, untreated sand used primarily in construction

20% Perlite

Planting—Green Side Up!
OK, There Might be a Little More to it Than That. . .

Seeds

Correct sowing depth is important, because if the seeds are sown too deep, they will just rot. If seeds are not planted deep enough, they will not germinate. Remember that seeds should generally be planted at a depth equal to its longest side. For the most part, though, just follow the instructions on the back of the seed packet.

Thinning is very important, because otherwise you end up with scraggly produce. But, I feel kind of mean when I thin plants since all the plants look equally healthy. How should I decide which plants live and which die? Plus, thinning is tedious and just another job to do. To avoid needing to thin plants, I mix tiny seeds with sand so as I sprinkle the seeds in a row, the seeds are more spread out.

A Warning about "Wildflower" Seed Mixes

A lot of novices are wooed by "convenient" wildflower seed mixes. First of all, if someone is calling them "wildflowers" and cannot identify where they are native to, they are either novices themselves or are purposely marketing to novices. Sure, it takes two seconds for you to scatter the seeds, but then what? How in the world are you going to be able to tell what is a weed and what is a plant? Also, these seed mixes generally do not contain seeds from local plants, so they may not be hardy (meaning they may not survive the winter). Not to mention that these seeds do not preserve the genetic diversity of your area, because they are not from the local ecotype. Next, the packet typically doesn't even list what is contained within it, so you can't even use the process of elimination to figure out what you've planted. Furthermore, these wretched mixes often weed species. Some are even invasive and/or noxious weeds. A noxious weed is a weed that is illegal to have on your property and if you have it on your property, it must be controlled. I have never heard of a case where people are hauled off to the big house for these offenses, but perhaps they should be. Invasive plants are a huge problem as mentioned in Chapter 3.

Seed mixes from reputable local companies, on the other hand, are completely appropriate if you have large areas to plant and you are seeking the "prairie look." You may need to burn and/or have professionals come in and help weed and burn it for you. Burning works to suppress weeds in native plantings because native prairie plants have evolved to withstand wildfires by putting a good share of their energy into their roots, so they can spring back to life after fires sweep through. Weeds, in contrast, are usually from other places of the world and do not generally have this long root adaptation.

Plant in rows, or if you are trying to achieve a more grouped English cottage look, plant groupings in staggered rows. Pretty soon these plants will fill themselves in so it won't look as if they are lined up for a choir concert. If you stick to this method, weeding will be easy. It's just like Sesame Street: "One of these things is not like the others. Which one is different? Do you know? ..."

Planting Plugs and Plants in Pots

Plugs are little plants about 3-9 inches high that are typically sold in four-packs or six-packs. Aside from starting plants by seed, plugs are the next most economical way to plant native plants. They are usually around a dollar per plant, and they will be nearly fully grown by the end of the growing season. When planting, make sure the top of the root ball is completely covered with soil. Otherwise, it will dry out and die within days. If you have a lot of plugs to plant, you may want to consider two tools. A bulb planter is an open-ended cylinder that is about four inches in diameter with a handle that you push into the soil and twist. As you pull it up, a big chunk of soil is inside the cylinder. Then you set your plant in the hole and poke the soil out of the bulb planter back into the hole. A bulb auger is another planting tool that you can attach to your cordless drill. It is coiled like a mini ice auger. An auger is good to use if you have a two-person planting team. One person goes along and drills, leaving a marker where the soil has been loosened up. The other person pulls the loose dirt back with a hand spade, pops in the plant, and covers it up. For planting larger plants in pots, a shovel is typically the best tool because it's better to err on the side of loosening up more soil than too little when digging the hole.

When planting any plant, it is important to examine the roots before planting and make sure they aren't encircling. If the roots are choking themselves and wrapping around in circles, correct the roots before planting. With plugs this would most likely mean tearing off the very bottom of the root ball and separating the roots so they are apt to grow out into the soil instead of continuing to grow in circles. With larger plants, this generally means "scoring" the root ball by taking a utility knife and making four vertical slashes on each side and an "X" on the bottom. Water your plants with a slow trickle after they are planted. If the soil settles, you may need to add a little more soil.

Planting Trees

Whereas care must be taken to make sure plants are planted deep enough, the opposite is true for trees. A big problem for trees is that they are planted too deep.[30] There has been loads of research in this area over the past fifteen years, but too many nurseries and installers are still lagging in their practices. Container trees (trees in big pots) are often planted too deep in their containers so a person needs to dig down to find the lateral roots (roots extending horizontally from the trunk) and make sure the lateral roots are just below the soil when planted.

Balled and burlap (B&B) trees are a pain in the back. They weigh hundreds of pounds and you need about three strong people and "ball hooks" (or haying hooks) to lift them into the hole. Also, they are dang near impossible to get out of the burlap without destroying the root ball. I say avoid them. Many contractors leave the wire cage and/or burlap on the tree claiming the burlap will decompose. This is just plain wrong and indefensible. Air is needed for decomposition. Sure, the tree will live in the soil it came in for a number of years, but eventually it will die—probably shortly after the warranty expires.

---

30   Ohio Department of Natural Resources, *The Perils of Planting Trees Too Deeply*, http://ohiodnr.com/forestry/urban/features/treeplanting/tabid/5462/Default.aspx (2013).

chapter ten

Tending Your Garden

Weed Identification, Chemical Use, Watering, Dividing and Trimming

Finding the Imposters - Weed Identification

Oʜ ᴍʏ! The garden is growing. Now what? Which plants are weeds? Identification of which plants you want growing in your garden versus those you don't will be easier if you followed the tips in the last chapter. However, even in my own garden, it seems most years I have a couple of mystery plants, and I'm left trying to figure out if they are invited guests or party crashers.

"Natural" versus "Native"

As I have mentioned, invasive plants are a serious problem, and they cause habitat degradation. Well-meaning people may allow areas in their yard to go "natural", deciding against mowing or spraying weeds. By taking this approach, however, they may not be doing nature any favors! Remember, there are many invasive weeds that must be controlled by law if they end up on your property. It is important to be able to identify the vegetation on your property, since not controlling invasive weeds can have a devastating impact on the environment.

Here are some nifty resources to help identify weeds.

- University of Minnesota–Extension website, "Is this plant a weed?" It's a great tool that is easy to use. http://www.extension. umn.edu/garden/yard-garden/
- Department of Natural Resources website, Invasive Species in Minnesota, http://www.dnr.state.mn.us/invasives/index.html
- *Common Lake Shore Weeds: A Guide for I.D. and Control in Lake Shore Buffers, Raingardens and any Native Planting, Second Edition.* To order a copy, contact the Sherburne Soil and Water Conservation District, http://www.sherburneswcd.org
- Otherwise, call your local watershed district, conservation district, city forester or county Master Gardener's help line for assistance. There are a lot of people who are very willing to help.

Should I Apply Weed-Killer (Herbicide)?

I am not against using organic and/or synthetic chemicals when a situation calls for it; for example, controlling illegal invasive plants. However, I think people spray too many chemicals in hopes of avoiding a little labor, thereby putting safety at risk. First, let's talk about the environmental impact of organic and synthetic chemicals. There is a perception that just because something is "natural" or "organic" that it is safe. Please take a minute to stop and think about the absurdity of this assumption. For example, arsenic (used in rat poison) is a naturally occurring chemical element that could possibly be labeled as "natural".

Understanding environmental impact quotients (EIQs) is key to evaluating the dangers organic and synthetic herbicides and pesticides may pose to humans and the environment. These quotients are made up of three parts: risk to the person applying poison, risk to consumer, and risk to the environment. The highest EIQs are around 100 and the lowest around 10. The higher the number, the greater the risk. EIQs are not currently listed on pesticide and herbicide packages. It would be great, however, if consumers pushed the industry to include EIQs on packaging to help well-meaning consumers avoid getting sucked into the "green" marketing of products. In the meantime, you can utilize Cornell University's calculator tool on their website: http://www.ny-sipm.cornell.edu/EIQCalc/input.php. Another indicator is, of course, the level of caution on the label. If the label says DANGER, you know it has a very high EIQ. WARNING indicates the level of EIQs is most likely in the middle. CAUTION means the product is on the lower end of the EIQ scale.

We live in a society accustomed to instant gratification. I realize this often when I volunteer for the Master Gardener's Yard and Garden phone line, where residents leave voicemail messages with questions about gardening. Nearly every time I take a shift, there are several calls that start out with, "What can I spray..." Sigh. Before resorting to spraying, please make sure you're doing everything you can to prevent the need to spray bugs and weeds.

How Do I Prevent Weeds?

Mulch is the best method for controlling weeds. Organic mulch, such as wood chips, also breaks down to help revitalize your soil. (NOTE: Be careful not to mulch every square inch because docile, solitary native bees need loose bare soil so they can lay their eggs.)

Another option is to use a pre-emergent herbicide (substance that inhibits the growth of weeds) such as corn gluten meal. This is generally considered safe, but it is pretty expensive and needs to be applied often. And keep in mind that if you want your little perennials to spread out and fill in, corn gluten meal may work against your goals and suppress the desired plants from re-seeding too.

In general, the best way to control weeds is to just pull the dang things yourself. There are countless homemade concoctions (garlic oil, clove oil, vinegar, salt, borax, torching weeds with a propane torch) and products for sale, but there are drawbacks to all of these methods and the bottom line is that they don't really reduce your labor. You still need to mix it up and go out and deal with each weed individually with the added concern of harming the plants you want to keep. Not to mention, many of these seemingly harmless concoctions have surprisingly high EIQs, and build up in your soil.

If your weeds have gone to seed, you may not want to compost them at home. In theory, your compost bin should reach a temperature hot enough to kill those seeds, but without professional equipment, it's pretty tough to know for sure. It's a downer to think about unknowingly planting weed seeds next time you use your finished compost.

What Do I Do with this Big Patch of Weeds?

Do you have an area so full of weeds that you just need to annihilate it and start over? It happens. Here are two methods that can be used in these situations.

Solarization (smothering with plastic)

This method is effective for patient people. Cover the weed patch with thin, clear plastic, taking care to tightly pin down the plastic with rocks, bricks, or tent stakes. The plastic covering creates a little greenhouse, baking the plants. Then, hope for a scorcher of a summer and be prepared to wait 4-6 weeks. Be aware that you will kill the organisms in the soil too. If you have disease problems, this will be great because you will be killing those too. Otherwise, it can cause growing problems later on, because you'll be eradicating many beneficial microorganisms in the soil too. Bummer. Either way, before planting, you'll want to add compost to boost the soil health and reintroduce our helpful but unseen microorganisms.

Broad-spectrum (Kills Most Everything) Weed Killers—like Roundup

Perhaps surprisingly, glyphosate (trademark name Roundup) has a low EIQ of 15.3 and is typically the chemical of choice used by restoration specialists who rid landscapes of harmful invasives before restoring them with native plants. Roundup works within days and areas where it's been applied are safe to plant soon after because the herbicide breaks down quickly. Obviously, follow the directions on the package, don't use it in the wind or rain, or when plants are blooming, and be careful not to use it anywhere near water. It is extremely harmful to frogs and fish.

How Do I Get Rid of Buckthorn, Exotic Honeysuckle, and Poison Ivy?

These weeds warrant serious action. The risk of doing nothing is greater than the risk of a blitzkrieg with triclopyr (trademark names Garlon, Weed B Gon). This chemical has an EIQ of 15–20, but is known to be carcinogenic.[31] To find out what is topping the invasive species list around you and warrants serious action, visit: http://www.fs.fed.us/invasivespecies/index.shtml or your local Department of Natural Resources. In Minnesota, the link is http://www.dnr.state.mn.us/invasives/index.html

Fertilizing

Simple! Don't. As long as you use compost in your soil, your plants will have adequate nutrition and won't need to be fertilized.[32] There are a number of drawbacks to using fertilizer as Jeff Gillman describes. (Gillman is an author and former Associate Professor in the Department of Horticultural Science at the University of Minnesota. Currently he is an instructor at Central Piedmont Community College in Charlotte North Carolina.)

The elements of synthetic fertilizers may come from mines that are destructive to the earth. The creation of synthetic nitrogen fertilizers uses a great deal of energy, which may be considered wasteful. Constant reapplication of synthetic fertilizers could change the natural balance of soil organisms.[33]

31   Jeff Gillman, *The Truth About Organic Gardening*, (Portland: Timber Press, 2008), 62.

32   Jeff Gillman, *The Truth About Organic Gardening*, (Portland: Timber Press, 2008), 30.

33   Jeff Gillman, *The Truth About Organic Gardening*, (Portland: Timber Press, 2008), 42.

Watering

Whereas I am not a proponent of watering grass and ornamental plants, I totally justify watering functional plants such as food, herbs and new native plantings. If you're not doing the watering of your food, some other farmer would be with the added environmental food mile costs as discussed in Chapter Three.

When to Water

The best time to water is early in the morning, at around 5:00 a.m. The cooler temperatures and calm conditions at this early hour mean water is not lost to evaporation. In addition, leaves won't stay wet too long. If you water in the evening, you increase the risk of fungal diseases because leaves dry more slowly (if at all) at night. If you are still reeling about the thought of getting up at 5:00 a.m. just to water plants, don't worry. This is written by a lawn chair gardener, remember? Just use a timer that hooks between your spigot and hose and will automatically turn on your sprinklers. There are tons of timers on the market. The simplest mechanical timers are less than ten dollars but have few programming options. More expensive ones have multiple programming options that allow you to water multiple times per day, on certain days of the week, etc.

How Much to Water

As a general guideline, provide about an inch of water each week or wet the soil to a depth of five or six inches. Use a rain gauge to help figure out how long it takes for your sprinkler to provide an inch of rain and then check a couple areas to see how far down into the soil the water has saturated. To check soil saturation, jab a hand spade into the ground and rock it back and forth to create a little pocket, then stick your hand in the hole and test for moisture. After you know how long it takes for your sprinkler to adequately water your garden soil to a depth of five to six inches, you can just set the timer for that amount of time at a certain time of day on certain days. To avoid being one of "those people" who wastefully waters in the rain, keep an eye on the weather and just turn off your sprinkler when it looks as if Mother Nature is going to water for you.

If you live in an area with sandy soil, you'll probably need to water gardens at least twice a week; three or more times in extreme heat. If your soil is loamy, a thorough watering once a week should suffice in all but the hottest weather when you may have to water every four or five days. Compacted clay soil is a bit more problematic. Water usually puddles before sprinklers deliver a sufficient quantity to encourage deep roots. Stop watering whenever the soil can't absorb more, then start again an hour or two later, until you've watered deeply enough. But, hopefully you won't have to deal with this because you will have already amended the soil.

Dividing and Trimming Plants

When to Divide Plants

Perennials are great because many of them grow in clumps that keep expanding. Eventually you may want to divide them and plant them elsewhere or give them to people. Sometimes you need to divide perennials because they develop a goofy looking bald spot in the middle like a donut. I break rules and divide plants whenever it's convenient for me. I cannot recall ever losing any as a result. However, if you want to be nice to your plants, consider dividing when it's not too hot or windy so they don't dry out. Also, divide flowers after they are done blooming so they have maximum time to recuperate before they are expected to bloom for you again.

How to Divide a Plant

Use a rounded shovel and make a clean slice through the middle of the plant (assuming you're dividing it in two). Then insert the tip of the shovel a few inches outside the perimeter of the plant, sink the shovel into the soil, and pop the plant out of the ground. Have the hole (or the pot) where you're planning to transplant the perennial ready so that the plant isn't exposed to drying elements for any length of time. If you can't replant it right away, place it in a large enough pot, and keep it well watered.

Trimming and Pruning

Similar to dividing plants, the rule of thumb for pruning or trimming established plants is do it right after the plant flowers so it has nearly a whole year to get ready to bloom again. If you trim a plant before it's supposed to bloom, you'll cut the blooms right off. Avoid pruning any new plants that have been planted during the current growing season. These newcomers just need to put down roots and get settled. Also, remember not to trim off more than one-third of the plant, since the leaves are needed to "feed" the plant through photosynthesis.

chapter eleven

Defending Your Garden

Deterring Insects, Diseases and Animals

IF YOUR FIRST REACTION IS TO KILL BUGS, you're not alone. But I urge you to put down the bottle of insecticide and step away before you do anything you might regret. Let's remind ourselves that insects do more good in the world than bad, and few insects need to be controlled. Please remember that insects—such as bees, butterflies, lacewings, wasps, tachinid flies, etc.—pollinate our food. We should be thanking a pollinator during each meal, since about every third bite of food is thanks to a pollinator.[34] The value of good nutrition is pretty tough to quantify, but the crops (fruits, vegetables, nuts) alone are worth around 20 billion dollars. Of course, insects also provide other products such as silk, lac (ingredient in floor and shoe polishes, insulators, various sealants, printing inks, and varnish), beeswax (base for ointments, polishes, candle making, lotions, creams, and lipsticks) as well as dyes. To boot, fruit flies have long been used in genetic studies. Another little known, interesting service offered by insects: some museums rely on a species of small beetle to clean skeletons.[35] Weird.

---

34   Tom Van Arsdall, Sunny Boyd, Pollinator Partnership, http://www.pollinator.org/PDFs/NPW.pdf (June 2010).

35   Smithsonian Institution, Benefits of Insects Information Sheet No. 72, http://www.si.edu/Encyclopedia_SI/nmnh/buginfo/benefits.htm (May 1999).

So when you meet a bug in your garden, please identify the bug as friend, foe, or just a nuisance before you take any action. Most likely, no action will be needed and you can go back to your lawn chair and relax. Most plants can tolerate losing about one-third of their leaves before they really start to suffer and slow down in their fruit bearing. Be forewarned that if you use a broad-spectrum insecticide, you will also kill the beneficial insects. Once the good guys are gone, nothing can stop attacks by the bad guys except using more pesticides. This is a dangerous and vicious cycle.

Floating row covers (thin garden fabric or even old curtain sheers) can prevent insects from attacking your plants. They are particularly useful for vegetable crops such as broccoli or squash. If the white moths can't lay their eggs on your plants, you won't have any of their little green worms hiding amongst the broccoli florets. Similarly, squash bugs can't reach squash plants that are nestled beneath floating row covers. But make sure to remove the fabric from the plants when they begin to flower so pollinating insects (a.k.a. the "good guys") can reach the blossoms.

Beneficial Bugs: Beyond Pollinators

I find it amazing that plants and beneficial insects communicate. When a plant is attacked by a harmful insect, the plant releases chemical signals into the air to lure the type of beneficial insect most likely to help it with its pest problem. Many beneficial insects leave a "footprint" signaling to other beneficial insects that they've already done the job of parasitizing the pest. Beneficial insects will also only lay eggs if pests are present in high enough numbers to feed their young. This is another reason not to get hasty with the pesticides. If we kill all the bad guys, the good guys won't reproduce. Who are the good guys? Imagine these bugs wearing little super-hero capes. If you see these bugs in your garden, leave them be!

- Aphidius wasp
- Assassin bug
- Big-eyed bug
- Damsel bug
- Ground beetle
- Hover fly
- Lacewing
- Ladybug
- Minute pirate bug
- Parasitic wasp
- Praying mantis
- Robber fly
- Spiders
- Tachinid fly

Invasive Species

Here I go again. Why do I have such a vengeance against alien plants, insects, and animals? Because they can harm the economy, environment, and/or humans. To underscore the evils of invasive species, consider that more than 135 billion dollars are spent combating invasive species in the United States each year. Therefore, when you have invasive species encroaching on your neighborhood, war on those species is warranted. An ounce of poison in a surprise ambush now, will most likely prevent trench warfare later. (Although remember to avoid the chemicals labeled "DANGER" if possible!)

Show No Mercy—Control-Worthy Bugs

- Brown Marmorated Stink bug
- Brown Spruce Long-horned Beetle
- Chinese Long-horned Beetle
- Emerald ash borer
- European and marsh crane flies
- European Grapevine Moth
- Gypsy moth
- Light Brown Apple Moth
- Sirex Wood Wasp
- Viburnum Leaf Beetle

Who Goes There? How Do You Identify What You're Looking At?

If I were to attempt to list and identify all of the bugs that you might encounter in your garden, this section could turn into a reference guide in a hurry. Some of my favorite reference guides and resources are:

- http://www.bugwood.org/
- http://www.extension.umn.edu/garden/ "What's wrong with my plant?" and "What insect is this?"

- I also like the book *Good Bug Bad Bug: Who's Who, What They Do, and How to Manage Them Organically (All You Need to Know about the Insects in Your Garden)*, by Jessica Walliser. It's informative and easy to use.
- Your local extension office

To help you figure out if you have an invasive species on your hands, these links might help you.

State Links

- Minnesota Department of Agriculture: http://www.mda.state.mn.us/plants/pestmanagement/invasivesunit.aspx
- Minnesota Sea Grant: http://www.seagrant.umn.edu/

National Links

- National Invasive Species Council: http://www.invasivespecies.gov/
- USGS Nonindigenous Aquatic Species: http://nas.er.usgs.gov/
- Protect Your Waters and Stop Aquatic Hitchhikers: http://www.protectyourwaters.net/

Cute Bunnies Bring Out Mean Ol' Mr. McGregor in Gardeners

As soon as you plant your garden, you might undergo a transformation from, "Ooh, look at the cute little bunny!" to thinking like Elmer Fudd, "Ah, those nasty wabbits!"

Rabbit damage is easy to identify because it will look like someone took a sharp scissors to your plant and cut it at a 45-degree angle. Bark damage is recognized by side-by-side teeth marks in the wood usually a ½-inch or more across (smaller teeth marks are more likely voles). The damage is typically eighteen inches or less from the ground where they can reach, but might be higher if there was a lot of snow. Rabbits prefer trees with thin bark—like fruit trees and maples—but will try almost any tree in a severe winter or if populations are high. Other signs include tracks and small, round, pea-sized droppings.

Rabbit Fence

Exclusion is the key to keeping bunnies out of the garden. Unfortunately, we're pretty much stuck using ugly wire mesh or ugly plastic mesh with one-inch holes, 18 to 24 inches high. The holes can't be any bigger than a baby bunny's head. If the bunny can stick its head through, it can get its whole body through. I use a green fence that isn't very visible, but I am searching for a decorative fence that also keeps out rabbits. (If you know of one on the market, let me know!) The fence should be installed tight against the ground or be buried a few inches deep to prevent the rabbits from digging underneath. The best thing to protect individual trees and shrubs is a rabbit exclusion fence or cylinder. There are pre-made plastic tree cylinders that can be used on seedlings. Taste deterrents, such as soap or hot chili spray, can also be used as a short-term solution during the winter months. All of these taste deterrents and smelly sprays work to various degrees, but they get expensive and are a hassle to apply regularly.

Trimming shrubs up from the ground and removing woodpiles reduces hiding spaces. Trapping can temporarily reduce the numbers of rabbits—until rabbits from surrounding areas move in. In general, most urban and suburban areas are ideal habitat for rabbits: plenty of food, cover, and few predators. In the long run, fencing is also the best way to protect trees and shrubs.

Oh, Dear! Deer.

My neighborhood, like many Midwestern suburbs, is surrounded by beautiful wetlands. I value wetlands. I understand they are like giant kidneys filtering our water, sponges that absorb flooding, and are resting and nesting spots for wildlife. They also provide food, habitat, and cover, not to mention generate revenue from eco-tourism activities like hunting, fishing, bird-watching, and photography. An acre of wetland can store 1–1.5 million gallons of floodwater. About half of our bird species nest or feed in wetlands. Although wetlands total only 5 percent of land surface in the United States, they are home to 31 percent of our plant species. Seventy-five percent of commercially harvested fish are wetland-dependent. If you add shellfish species, that number jumps to 95 percent.[36]

But these wetlands also house herds of deer that carouse about neighborhoods at dawn and dusk. Yes, they are like gangs in my neighborhood. They are brazen enough to walk right down the middle of the street in the wee hours of the morning. And they take full advantage of the sidewalks and pedestrian crossings in deep snow.

Fences definitely reduce deer activity, though they're not 100 percent effective. For a small garden patch, use a four-foot high fence. Deer avoid small, penned-in sites. For a larger garden, deer will jump a vertical wood fence eight feet high. Dang. A six-foot high fence made of wire, not wood, angled 30 degrees away from the yard creates both a psychological and physical barrier, because deer will hesitate to jump over something in which they fear becoming entangled. The question becomes, however, do you really want a weird looking six-foot wire fence angled at 30 degrees around the perimeter of your yard? Will you start to feel like your yard has become a prison? One of my favorite fencing methods is stringing fishing line at knee and chest height around narrow beds. My experience is that it is about 85 percent effective and it is barely noticeable.

---

36   United States Environmental Protection Agency, *Functions and Values of Wetlands*, EPA 843-F-01-002c, September 2001

Deer Deterrents

Deer deterrents work—for awhile—until the deer study the situation and realize the "scarecrow" motion sensor sprinkler, light or fake owl isn't a true threat. Suburban deer are notorious for figuring out decoys. My theory is that the deer have too much time on their hands since they don't even need to look too far for food with virtually endless landscaping buffets available for their choosing. And, to my knowledge, deer don't really have too many other hobbies. That leaves them with nothing better to do than to spy on our plants and figure out their plan of attack. I imagine the deer discussing in which yard they would like to dine for breakfast as people discuss going out to eat. "I am in the mood for fresh tomato plants," offers one. "Oh good idea, then we could head over to the tan house on the corner for some apples for dessert," replies the other deer.

Two basic types of deer repellents are available. Contact repellents are applied to the plants, causing them to taste bad. Area repellents are placed in the problem area and repel due to their foul odor. People have been known to mix up many different concoctions. Like the rabbit repellents, they all work to varying degrees, but you need to reapply them often, especially in rainy weather. Again, many are smelly—they repel people—and are a hassle to apply. Another problem I've experienced with repellents is that I didn't really know when I needed to reapply until the damage had been done. The directions say to reapply after rain. How much rain? What if there is a dry spell? Do you need to reapply then?

Birds, Squirrels and Other Animals

Netting can be set up around specific plants. I have netting around my blueberry bushes all year round. The netting is reusable for several years. Allowing some space in building your netting cage is helpful so the leaves don't grow through the netting.

Acceptance

Acceptance is key to many aspects of a happy life. I do some fencing, but I have just accepted that I will be sharing my plants with the wildlife around my house to some extent. A person could drive themselves crazy otherwise. I also have some "sacrificial plants." There were some pretty ugly hostas in my yard when we moved in. The deer like them and they can have them.

Diseases

Diseases are too numerous and too diverse to cover at length in this little book. Here are some quick tips for handling them.

1. Prevention is best. As with people, it's best to prevent disease on plants. Good watering practices and making sure your plants have ample space between them will prevent many fungal diseases. As with the prevention of insect damage, this is another instance where using

the intercropping or companion planting method is beneficial, as it can prevent diseases from finding like plants.

2. Make a quick visit to your garden often to detect and yank sick plants before disease spreads. If you see a plant that looks diseased, pick off the affected leaves or, if necessary, pull the whole plant to keep it from spreading to other plants. Typically, that will be the end of the problem.

3. If disease is a reoccurring problem, or you have an inquiring mind, bring in a sample to your university extension's diagnostic clinic. For plants, bring a sample about 8–10 inches long, making sure to include leaves, flowers, and fruit if available. Include both healthy and damaged material. For disease/insect problems, note if some or all of your plants are affected. Note where on the plant the problem occurs (for example, on lower branches of a tree, random branches, etc.) Is the problem spreading? Bring photos of the diseased plants. If insects are part of the problem, place some in a container and put it in the freezer to preserve them.

chapter twelve

Get Your Lawn Chair Out

Relax and Enjoy!

GRAB A REFRESHING BEVERAGE, sit down, relax, and close your eyes.

Drink in the beauty.

Take a deep breath.

Exhale s-l-o-w-l-y.

Enjoy the peace.

Celebrate that you are through with the tiring treadmill of watering your lawn only to make it grow faster causing it to need more frequent mowing. Maybe even gloat a bit because lawn chair gardeners have time to sit and enjoy their gardens.

Doesn't it feel good to know that your lovely garden isn't just a "show horse," but a functional "work horse" too? However large or small, tidy or untidy, your garden provides a multitude of benefits that extend into the future. It is my hope that you will feel a deepened sense of serenity knowing that your garden is making a positive impact for future generations who will cherish the clean, abundant water you have helped conserve. Not only people, but I bet critters, insects, and song birds would also thank you for the habitat if they could.

As you survey your garden, go ahead and give yourself a pat on the back for a job well done. That's right, WELL DONE! Your garden doesn't need to be perfect to be enjoyable. Since gardens have so many "moving parts," a perfect garden is virtually unattainable. There will inevitably be an unfortunate bare spot or a plant that doesn't stand as you'd like it to even with staking and supports. But, if you wait until it's "perfect," you will deprive yourself of enjoyment. So, go ahead and invite people over to enjoy your garden with you. Don't miss opportunities to enjoy time with loved ones because you are waiting for a day that may never come.

chapter thirteen

Getting Away with Doing (Almost) Nothing

Fall and/or Spring Clean-Up

Pᴇᴏᴘʟᴇ ᴛᴀʟᴋ about maintenance like it's some looming, mysterious task. I don't understand this because I look at perennial garden maintenance this way: simply whack it down and rake it up, The most important part of this process is timing. Take a look at your schedule and try to figure out what's going to work best for you. Are you having a baby due on March 31st (like I did last year)? That will make it tough to get out early in the spring. Another year, I was too pregnant in the spring and early summer to bend over. I didn't get out to the garden until the end of August. That's the beauty of a native garden—it is like an old friend who understands that sometimes you just don't have time to have daily contact even though you'd like to. Remember, this book is for lawn chair gardeners, so do what works for you. However, if it's all the same to you, it's most beneficial to wildlife to leave vegetation standing over the winter so birds and other animals can snack on the seeds and the beneficial insects can overwinter in the plant stems.

In October, I just yank out the annual vegetables (roots and all because they won't be surviving the winter). I also am sure to take out any vegetation that looks like it could harbor a disease or pathogen. To keep the garden looking nice into the fall, I also may cut back some of the flowers that look past their prime or are keeling over. If tree leaves have fallen into the perennial bed, I just leave them there until spring. Generally, snow is enough of a blanket to insulate perennials, but our snowfall amounts are so unpredictable that a little extra leaf insulation doesn't hurt. If, however, the leaves are blowing around and may become my neighbor's problem or blow into the street, I rake them up. (Remember from Chapter 3 that leaves and grass clippings are a major source of water pollution.)

In April, I go out with a string trimmer or a hedge trimmer for thick-stemmed plants and whack all of the perennials down. This is fun! It gives me such a feeling of power as I annihilate the plants down to a couple of inches. Then I rake the leaves and stems onto a big tarp. I like using a metal leaf rake (the older, the better) because it has more give. Plastic leaf rakes and garden rakes pull the plants completely out of the ground. Then I fold the tarp up like a giant burrito and stick it into the back of my car to take to the county compost site or I stick it into the big receptacle for the waste haulers to take to the compost site. That's it. It's not rocket science.

chapter fourteen

Tipping the Scales

Goodbye Ornamentals,
H-E-L-L-O Functional Yards!
It's Time for Yard 2.0

For centuries lawns have served as status symbols; only the wealthy could afford to waste space and not use the land to produce food. And, only the wealthy could afford to hire a small army to scythe it. Although the lawn started as a sign of upper-class wealth, it has become a symbol of the middle-class American dream: a home of one's own, surrounded by green grass. After a couple hundred years of this revered lawn aesthetic, I think it's time we adopt a "Yard 2.0" that reflects the environmental and social issues of our times.

Picture a world where habitat for native critters was restored through diverse native plant communities and neighborhoods doubled as wildlife corridors. Consider how nice it would be if pesticides weren't commonplace and people simply planted native plants to bring in beneficial insects to control the pests. What a wonderful world it would be if planting for clean water were the norm rather than the exception. Wouldn't it be nice if we took our shallowly-rooted lawns off of life-support? How would the world look if no-mow ground covers that could find their own water were planted in our play spaces instead lawn grass?

What if our yards worked for us and paid us in produce? I would love to live in a world where families with standard quarter-acre lots would plant a row for the hungry and donate extra produce to those in need. I would also enjoy living in a community where new neighbors were welcomed with planting parties and harvests were shared with each other. Imagine if everyone ate a healthy diet with plenty of locally grown, fresh vegetables and obesity and diabetes were diminished. What if the slow food movement (where people cook at home) gained traction and surpassed fast food? What if all children understood where their food came from?

Suppose people stayed in shape by working in their gardens. Imagine a world where we could feel like we were doing everything possible to slow the pace global warming; a world where we could honestly look our kids right in the eyes and say it's going to be okay. Together, we can turn these aspirations into reality and achieve a more balanced world, one meal and one yard at a time.

As we close the first two sections of this book reviewing philosophical and moral aspects of gardening as well as how-to information, it is my hope that you embark on the rewarding path of lawn chair gardening. Along your journey, may you find balance, joy, satisfaction, and a renewed connection with the environment. Perhaps you will also feel comfort in knowing that you are helping to tip the scales in favor of a more balanced world. Imagine! It could be your garden that tips the scales and is the impetus behind changing the status quo of ornamental yards to functional yards. Goodbye ornamentals, hello functional yards.

chapter fifteen

Harvest and Cook

Simple Meals

I STARTED OUT AS A VEGETABLE GARDENER, but I quickly converted to native flowers because, at that time, I didn't really cook and I didn't like the pressure of eating six tomatoes for dinner. Now, of course, I love to grow both edibles and natives and I've figured out how to freeze surpluses. I am including this recipe section just in case there are others who fall into the "Now what do I do with all of this produce?" category. I actually enjoy cooking now, and feel good about serving my family healthy meals that have less of an environmental footprint.

A friend once told me that the key to learning to cook was having a decent knife. I dismissed the advice as being somewhat snooty. After all, her husband was a head chef in a four-star restaurant where Oprah would dine when she came to town. Now I completely agree and see the wisdom in my friend's simple advice. Since good, healthy food involves using fresh ingredients, you are going to need to cut up those ingredients. It's pretty unavoidable. I tried all kinds of choppers looking for a perfect, time-saving cutting tool. But I found you still have to use a knife to cut the vegetable into the right size to fit the various choppers, and, to boot, the chopping devices were all a bit troublesome to clean. We have several good knives, but I could get by with just one Santoku knife. So, if you don't have a good Santoku knife, put this book down and go get one (and be sure to keep it sharp).

On my website (http://www.lawnchairgardener.com/recipes)

you will find my downloadable meal planner and grocery list templates (pictured on page 117). Are these templates sophisticated? Nope. There are fancy apps galore for meal planning and list making, and if you are adept at using these apps efficiently, I am impressed! For others, like me, who find it not any faster to look at a little screen and poke around, you might find these simple little templates useful. Either my husband or I sit down for about fifteen minutes per week to write up the meal plan. We do this by looking through our favorite cookbooks and/or looking back at our completed monthly meal plans. We then write down the recipe name, the cookbook it's from and page number for each day of the week ahead. As I pick out my recipes, I jot down on the shopping list what we need to purchase to make the recipe. I have the shopping list organized according to the layout of the store where I shop most frequently, so I don't have to do any back tracking. It's great because I don't have to wrack my brain about what to make for dinner each night; I simply refer to my plan. I only have to think once.

If I call myself a lawn chair gardener, I am a self-proclaimed "arm chair" cook. I tend to make pretty simple meals and my programmable slow cooker is pretty much my best friend. If I am working or busy on a particular day, I know that my plug-in butler will have dinner ready for me when I get home. If I have to leave really early in the morning, I cut up the vegetables and do the other prep work the night before so it's ready to put into the slow cooker before I leave the next morning.

I have one cautionary tale about the slower cooker. To save time, my wonderful, helpful husband and I prepared a meal the night before and put everything right into the crock and we put the crock in the fridge. Then, all we had to do the following morning was take out the crock, throw it into the cooker and turn it on. Why didn't we think of this magnificent time-saving trick before? We congratulated ourselves for our ingenuity. However, we soon found that the difference in temperature between fridge and slow cooker caused the crock to crack. Even pausing to think that through for just a minute would've told us this was not a clever idea.

I read somewhere that most families have about a dozen meals they make over and over. That sounds a bit boring, doesn't it? The following recipes are ones that incorporate my homegrown edibles and are easy to make. I am, by no means, an expert chef, so I feel a little sheepish handing over my recipes. For those of you who enjoy cooking, I hope you will share your recipes with us at http://www.lawnchairgardener.com/recipes/.

Of course I prefer fresh or frozen ingredients whenever possible. However, sometimes the convenience of canned goods wins. For this reason, I've listed the ingredients both ways. Also, I prefer to use dried beans whenever possible because they contain less sodium and make less of an environmental footprint by not being packaged in a can. (It takes a lot of resources to produce a can and even to recycle it.)

I have included meat recipes, even though I realize that eating vegetarian consumes far fewer resources. I try to eat locally raised meat as much as possible to minimize our environmental footprint.

Finally, since my family is now virtually dairy-free due to my youngest son's mild allergy, many recipes include tips to alter recipes to accommodate dairy-free diets.

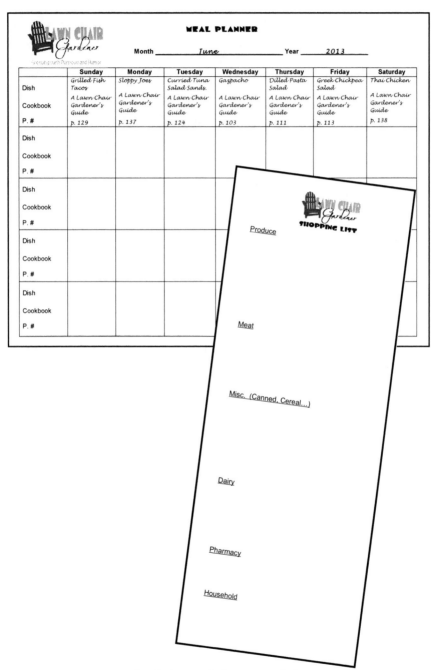

	Sunday	Monday	Tuesday	Wednesday	Thursday	Friday	Saturday
Dish	Grilled Fish Tacos	Sloppy Joes	Curried Tuna Salad Sands.	Gazpacho	Dilled Pasta Salad	Greek Chickpea Salad	Thai Chicken
Cookbook	A Lawn Chair Gardener's Guide	A Lawn Chair Gardener's Guide	A Lawn Chair Gardener's Guide	A Lawn Chair Gardener's Guide	A Lawn Chair Gardener's Guide	A Lawn Chair Gardener's Guide	A Lawn Chair Gardener's Guide
P. #	p. 129	p. 137	p. 124	p. 103	p. 111	p. 113	p. 138

MEAL PLANNER

Month _____ June _____ Year _____ 2013 _____

SHOPPING LIST

Produce

Meat

Misc. (Canned, Cereal...)

Dairy

Pharmacy

Household

Download the meal planner and shopping list at
http://www.lawnchairgardener.com/recipes/

Cheddar Squash Soup (can also be made dairy-free)

SERVES 6

1½ pounds butternut squash

¼ cup salted butter or 2-3 tablespoons olive oil

1 yellow onion, chopped

1 tablespoon peeled, grated fresh ginger

3½ cups vegetable or chicken stock

½ teaspoon pepper

1 cup half-and-half (or unsweetened cashew or almond milk)

6 ounces shredded sharp cheddar cheese (or just leave out if avoiding dairy)

3 thinly sliced green onions

Preheat oven to 350°F. Cut squash in half and remove the seeds. Place squash cut-side down on a cookie sheet. Fill the cookie sheet with a ¼ inch of water. Cook for about 40 minutes, or until the squash is easily pierced with a fork. Let the squash cool slightly, then scoop out the squash.

In a large stockpot, melt the butter (or olive oil) over moderate heat. Add onion and ginger and sauté for 5 minutes until onion is soft. Add stock, pepper, and squash. Bring to a boil over medium-high heat. Reduce heat to low and simmer covered for 15 minutes. Transfer soup to a blender and process until smooth. Return puree to the stockpot and add the half-and-half (or cashew/almond milk). Stir in cheese until melted (optional) and garnish with green onions.

Cheesy Broccoli Soup (can also be made dairy-free)

SERVES 4

2 tablespoons butter or olive oil

1 medium onion, chopped

2 cloves garlic, minced

4 cups broccoli florets (about a head)

2 medium Yukon gold potatoes

5 cups vegetable or chicken broth

1½ cups shredded cheddar cheese (optional)

½ cup buttermilk, cream (optional)

Salt and black pepper (to taste)

Melt the butter or olive oil in a large saucepan over medium heat. Add the onion and garlic and cook until softened, about 5 minutes.

Add the broccoli, potato, and broth. Raise the heat to high and let the broth come to a boil. Reduce heat, cover pan, and simmer until broccoli and potatoes are softened, about 10 minutes.

Let the broccoli mixture cool slightly then transfer it to a blender or food processor and puree the soup in batches.

Return the soup to the saucepan, add the cheese (optional) and buttermilk or cream (also optional). Milk substitutes may be used, but my family voted using a milk substitute. Skipping the milk and cheese to make the dairy-free option was more popular.

Cook the soup over low until the cheese melts, about 3 minutes. Make sure the soup does not come to a boil—buttermilk or cream may scald. Season with salt and pepper.

Gazpacho
SERVES 4 (1 cup servings)

1½ cups spicy V-8 juice

2 tablespoons lemon juice

1 tablespoon olive oil

½ teaspoon salt

¼ teaspoon red pepper sauce (or more to taste)

2 tomatoes, chopped

¾ cup chopped cucumber (set ¼ cup aside to use as accompaniment)

¾ cup chopped green pepper (set ¼ cup aside to use as accompaniment)

½ cup chopped onion (set ¼ cup aside to use as accompaniment)

1 cup seasoned croutons

Place all ingredients **except accompaniments and croutons** in blender, cover, and blend on medium speed until smooth. Refrigerate for about 4 hours. Serve garnished with accompaniments.

Leek Potato Soup

SERVES 6

1 pound leeks (about 3–5 medium leeks), cleaned, with dark green ends cut off

3 tablespoons unsalted butter

Heavy pinch of kosher salt, plus additional for seasoning

14 ounces (about 3 small) Yukon gold potatoes, peeled and diced

4 cups vegetable broth

1 cup heavy cream or half-and-half (optional)

1 cup buttermilk (optional)

½ teaspoon white pepper

1 tablespoon snipped chives

Chop the leeks into small pieces. In a 6-quart pot over medium heat, melt the butter. Add the leeks and a pinch of salt and sweat for 5 minutes. Decrease the heat to medium-low and cook until the leeks are tender, approximately 25 minutes, stirring occasionally.

Add the potatoes and the vegetable broth, increase the heat to medium-high, and bring to a boil. Reduce the heat to low, cover, and gently simmer until the potatoes are soft, approximately 45 minutes.

Let the mixture cool slightly then transfer it to a blender or food processor and puree the soup in batches. Stir in the cream, buttermilk, (optional) and pepper. This soup can be served hot or cold.

Lentil-Spinach Soup

SERVES 4 (1¼ cup servings)

4 medium onions, sliced

2 cloves garlic, finely chopped

4 tablespoons olive oil

6 cups water

2 teaspoons salt

16 ounces dried lentils (about 2½ cup)

2 teaspoons grated lemon peel

8 cups spinach chopped, or 1 package of frozen, chopped spinach

Combine everything in slow cooker and cook for 8 hours on high.

Navy Bean and Ham Soup

SERVES 7 (1 cup servings)

7 cups water
1 pound dried navy or pea beans (about 2 cups)
2 cups ham or a ham steak (no need to cut, will fall apart in slow cooker)
1 small onion, chopped
2-3 carrots, chopped
½ teaspoon salt
1 bay leaf
a dash of pepper

Combine everything in slow cooker and cook for 8 hours on high. Remove bay leaf before serving.

Pesto Tomato Soup

SERVES 4

3¼ cups chicken or vegetable stock

2 cups dried beans or 2 (14-ounce) cans white beans (i.e. Garbanzo, Canellini, Fazolia, White Kidney Bean, Great Northern), drained and rinsed

If you are using dried beans, soften them according to their package instructions.

4 tablespoons tomato paste

5 tablespoons pesto (Buy already prepared or make your own. See pesto recipe on page 149.)

Put the stock in a pan with the beans and bring to a boil.

Reduce the heat and stir in the tomato paste and pesto. Cook gently for 5 minutes.

Transfer about six ladlefuls of the soup to a blender or food processor, scooping up plenty of the beans. Process until smooth.

Return the puree to the pan. Heat gently, stirring frequently, for 5 minutes. Serve with warm, crusty bread or breadsticks.

Roasted Tomato-Basil Soup

Serves 6

3½ pounds peeled, whole tomatoes or two 28-ounce cans peeled whole tomatoes, with 3 cups liquid reserved

1 tablespoon olive oil

2½ tablespoons dark brown sugar, packed

1 medium onion, finely chopped

3 cups vegetable or chicken broth

3 tablespoons tomato paste

¼ teaspoon ground allspice

10-ounce can evaporated milk

¼ cup shredded fresh basil, shredded (about 10 large leaves)

Salt and black pepper to taste

Preheat oven to 450°F. Spray or brush baking sheet with olive oil or nonstick cooking spray. Arrange tomatoes on sheet in single layer. Sprinkle with brown sugar and top with onion. Bake for about 25 minutes, or until tomatoes look dry and light brown. Let tomatoes cool slightly then chop.

Place tomato mixture, 3 cups reserved liquid from tomatoes, broth, tomato paste, and allspice in a slow cooker. Mix. Cover and cook on low for 8 hours or on high for 4 hours.

Add evaporated milk and basil and season with salt and pepper. Cook on high for 30 minutes or until hot.

Split Pea Soup

SERVES 8 (1½ cup servings)

8 cups water

1 pound dried split peas (about 2¼ cups), rinsed and drained

2 pounds ham (no need to cut, will fall apart in slow cooker)

1 medium onion, chopped (about ½ cup)

¼ teaspoon pepper

2 medium carrots, sliced (about 1 cup)

2 medium stalks celery, sliced (about 1 cup)

1 teaspoon salt (I usually add this toward the end in case the ham is saltier than normal)

Put everything in slow cooker and cook for 8 hours on high.

Squash Bisque

SERVES 4

2 leeks, washed and coarsely chopped, tough greens discarded

1 large winter squash (butternut, buttercup, acorn, etc.)

3 cups chicken or vegetable stock

2 carrots, peeled and sliced

1 apple, peeled and chopped

1 Yukon gold potato, peeled and chopped

1 large onion, chopped

¼ cup parsley, chopped

2 cloves garlic

1 teaspoon dried oregano

½ teaspoon dried rosemary

½ teaspoon nutmeg

1 cup evaporated milk or half-in-half (or unsweetened almond or cashew milk)

Preheat oven to 350°F. Cut squash in half. Place squash cut-side down on a cookie sheet. Fill the cookie sheet with a ¼ inch of water. Cook for about 45 minutes, or until the squash is easily pierced with a fork. Let the squash cool slightly, then scoop out the squash or peel the skin off.

In a stock pot, combine all ingredients except for milk. Cover and cook over medium heat until vegetables are tender, about 30 minutes.

Puree in a blender, working in batches. Stir in milk, adding more if bisque is too thick.

 Salads

Dilled Pasta Salad

SERVES 8

2 cups Rotini or spiral macaroni

½ cup mayonnaise

¼ cup sour cream (or dairy-free sour cream)

1 tablespoon fresh dill weed (or ½ teaspoon dried dill weed)

½ teaspoon salt

½ teaspoon dry mustard

¼ teaspoon pepper

½ cup olives, pitted and sliced (any type of olives—I like Kalamata or green)

1 medium zucchini, thinly sliced

1 medium carrot, shredded

1 small onion, chopped (about ¼ cup)

Cook pasta according to package directions. Drain and set aside.

In a large bowl, combine mayonnaise, sour cream, dill weed, salt, mustard, and pepper. Add remaining ingredients and cooled pasta. Cover and refrigerate for at least 3 hours before serving.

Garbanzo Bean Salad

SERVES 4

4 ounces mushrooms

½ medium green pepper, cut in strips

½ cup pitted olives (green or Kalamata)

¼ cup sliced green onions

2 cup cooked garbanzo beans, drained

Lettuce leaves

2 small tomatoes, cut into wedges

½ cup plain yogurt (or dairy-free yogurt)

¼ cup mayonnaise

1½ teaspoons lemon juice

½ teaspoon cumin

¼ teaspoon garlic salt

⅛ teaspoon ground turmeric

Mix mushrooms, green pepper, olives, green onions, and garbanzo beans and refrigerate for a least 2 hours.

To make the dressing, combine yogurt, mayonnaise, lemon juice, cumin, garlic salt, and turmeric in a small bowl. Just before serving, toss salad with yogurt dressing. Serve on lettuce leaves and garnish with tomato wedges.

Greek Salad

SERVES 4-6

4 medium cucumbers

1 large red onion, sliced

2 cups tomatoes, coarsely chopped

½ cup extra-virgin olive oil

Juice of 2 lemons

8 ounces feta cheese, in blocks or crumbled

Salt and freshly ground pepper

Fresh oregano, chopped

Kalamata olives

Peel, seed and chop the cucumbers. (To seed, cut in half lengthwise and use a spoon to scoop out the seeds.) Put the chopped cucumbers in a serving bowl with the onion and tomatoes. Toss with olive oil and lemon juice. Top with feta. Add salt, pepper and oregano to taste.

Greek Chickpea Salad

SERVES 5 (1 cup servings)

4 cups packed spinach leaves (about 4 large handfuls)
1 cup canned chickpeas, rinsed and drained
¼ cup pitted Kalamata olives, sliced
1 large shallot or ¼ red onion
2 tablespoons crumbled feta cheese
¼ cup plain Greek yogurt
2 teaspoons white wine vinegar
1 clove garlic, minced
1 teaspoon olive oil
¼ teaspoon pepper
⅛ teaspoon salt

Combine spinach, chickpeas, olives, shallot, and feta in a large salad bowl.

To make the dressing, combine the remaining six ingredients. Let flavors blend for a few hours. Toss with salad shortly before serving.

Salad with Apples and Goat Cheese

SERVES 4-6

1 teaspoon butter (or margarine)

1 cup walnuts

¼ cup brown sugar

2 tablespoons water

¼ cup olive oil

½ cup balsamic vinegar

6–8 cups mixed greens

4–5 ounces soft goat cheese (There are cheese substitutes, but I don't recommend them for this recipe, unfortunately.)

4 apples, peeled, cored and sliced (Honeycrisp, Harrelson, or whatever you like)

Salt and freshly ground pepper

To toast the walnuts, place butter and walnuts in a skillet over medium-high heat. Stir constantly for about 5 minutes, making sure butter does not burn. Continue stirring until the walnuts are toasted. Add brown sugar and water, stirring constantly. The water will evaporate, leaving the nuts with a sugar coating. Remove from heat. Cool and set aside.

To prepare the dressing, mix the olive oil and balsamic vinegar. Set aside.

Toss the greens together. Assemble salads on individual plates. Add greens, goat cheese, walnuts, apples, dressing, salt, and pepper.

Waldorf Salad

SERVES 4-6

2 cups chopped apples (with skin on). Honeycrisp apples are particularly good in this recipe.

1½ teaspoons fresh lime juice

¼ cup chopped celery

¼ cup raisins or dried cranberries

3 tablespoons chopped walnuts

¼ cup vanilla yogurt (or non-dairy yogurt)

¼ cup whipped topping (i.e. Cool Whip)

½ teaspoon grated lime peel

⅛ teaspoon ground nutmeg

Place apples in a bowl. Sprinkle with the lime juice, then toss. Add the celery, raisins, and walnuts. In a separate bowl, combine remaining four ingredients. Add dressing to salad, mixing thoroughly.

Apple Chutney (Great on Turkey Burgers)

Makes 6–8 cups

15 tart apples, peeled, cored, and finely chopped
1 yellow onion, quartered
3 (1-inch) pieces fresh ginger root, peeled
1 cup white wine vinegar
½ cup white sugar
½ cup brown sugar
½ teaspoon cinnamon
½ teaspoon white pepper
½ teaspoon ground cardamom
¼ teaspoon ground nutmeg

Combine all ingredients in a saucepan and bring to a boil, reduce heat, and cover. Simmer 30 minutes, stirring frequently, until the apples are tender. Mix in a little water as necessary to keep the ingredients moist. Remove and discard the onion and ginger.

Store in the refrigerator until ready to serve or divide into several jars and store in the freezer to use as needed.

Basil Bruschetta

MAKES 16–18 APPETIZERS

2 cups fresh basil leaves

1 cup cherry tomatoes

½ cup ground cherries (optional)

1–2 small sweet peppers

2 garlic cloves, finely chopped

¾ cup extra virgin olive oil

½ cup grated Parmesan cheese

1 loaf French bread, sliced

Salt to taste

Chop basil, tomatoes, ground cherries, and peppers. Put the chopped vegetables in a bowl with the garlic. Add the olive oil. Stir in the cheese. Salt to taste.

Spoon the mixture over sliced bread and broil until the cheese melts and the bread is toasted. The mixture can also be served at room temperature as a dip with fresh bread.

Crispy Roasted Potatoes with Rosemary and Herbs

SERVES 4

6–8 potatoes with skins

Olive oil

Coarse salt

2–3 tablespoons fresh rosemary, chopped

2 tablespoons fresh thyme, chopped

Salt and ground pepper

Preheat oven to 400°F. Wash potatoes and cut off any bad spots. Cut into bite-size pieces but do not peel. Swirl a little olive oil in a roasting pan and add the potatoes. Stir to coat. Add the fresh herbs and stir. Sprinkle generously with salt and pepper. Roast in oven for 25–30 minutes, or until potatoes are hot and crispy.

Grandma Opal's Potato Salad

SERVES 8-10

8 medium potatoes, cooked and chopped (any kind)

½ cup sour cream (or dairy-free sour cream)

¾ cup real mayonnaise

2-4 teaspoons mustard

2 tablespoons sugar

¼ cup onion (or chives)

½ cup celery

1-2 tablespoons dill, chopped (optional)

2 tablespoons flat-leaf parsley, chopped (optional)

4 eggs, hard-boiled and peeled

Salt and pepper to taste

Wash, peel and chop the potatoes. (If you are using small red potatoes, you can leave the skins on.) Place potatoes in a pot and just cover with water. Boil until the potatoes are soft and easily pierced with a fork. Drain the water and set the potatoes aside to cool down.

In the serving bowl, combine sour cream, mayonnaise, mustard, sugar, onion, and celery. (Include dill and parsley if desired.) Add in potatoes and hard-boiled eggs carefully so they don't get smashed. Let the flavors blend several hours before serving.

Quick Spanakopita

SERVES 4

1 narrow loaf of French bread (about 24 inches long)

3 cups spinach, chopped

3-4 green onions, chopped

Small handful fresh, flat-leaf parsley, chopped

1 egg, beaten

4 ounces feta cheese

¼ teaspoon hot pepper flakes

Preheat oven to 350°F. Cut off top of French bread and hollow out the middle (reserve for making croutons another time). To make the filling, blend together the remaining ingredients. Place mixture in hollowed out bread. Bake for 20-30 minutes until filling is set and bread is golden brown.

Sandwiches

Bacon Lettuce Tomato (BLTs, BSTs, or BBTs)

Of course you don't need a recipe for the classic Bacon, Lettuce, and Tomato sandwich on lightly toasted bread with a thin layer of mayo. Yum. But perhaps you might like to try trading in the lettuce for spinach and/or basil instead.

Curried Tuna Salad Sandwiches

MAKES ABOUT 3 SANDWICHES

1 6½-ounce can tuna, water-packed, drained
1 celery stalk, finely chopped
1 green onion, finely sliced
Handful toasted chopped or sliced almonds
2 tablespoons raisins
¼ cup mayonnaise
2 teaspoons curry powder
6 slices bread, toasted

Mix all ingredients (except bread) together. Spread on toasted bread.

Egg Salad Sandwiches

Egg Salad with Dill
SERVES 3-4

6 hard-boiled eggs, chopped
2 ribs of celery, minced
¼ cup grated carrot
2 tablespoons chopped red onion or minced chives
2 tablespoons plain yogurt
2 tablespoons mayonnaise
2 teaspoons minced dill
2 teaspoons Dijon mustard
1 teaspoon lemon juice (optional)
Salt and black pepper
6 slices of bread

Mix all ingredients except bread together. Spread on toasted bread.

Egg Salad with Caramelized Onions
SERVES 4–6

1 tablespoon unsalted butter
1 cup onion, minced
6 large hard-boiled eggs, chopped
½ cup mayonnaise
¼ teaspoon salt
⅛ teaspoon black pepper
6–8 bread slices

Melt butter in a small frying pan over very low heat. Add onions and cook slowly for 15 minutes stirring often until golden brown and caramelized. Remove pan from heat and allow onions to cool. In a medium bowl, combine onion, chopped eggs, mayonnaise, salt, and pepper. Mix and chill. Serve on bread.

Main Dishes

Caramelized Shallots in Red Wine with Pasta

SERVES 6

1 pound pasta, uncooked
3-4 tablespoons extra-virgin olive oil
12-14 shallots, sliced lengthwise
½ cup red wine
Salt and freshly ground pepper
Parmesan cheese

To prepare shallots, cuts off ends and peel down until you get to the shiny purplish layer.

Heat oil in skillet. Sauté the shallots in the oil over medium low heat until they are caramelized (about an hour), flipping them about every 10-15 minutes. Stir in red wine and cooking for another 10 minutes.

Bring large pot of water to a boil, add pasta and cook as instructed by package.

Pour sauce over pasta and serve with Parmesan cheese.

Chicken Pot Pie

SERVES 8

IF TWO 10-INCH PIES SEEMS LIKE TOO MUCH, FREEZE A PIE FOR AN EASY DINNER LATER.

4 boneless, skinless chicken breasts, cooked

4 carrots, peeled and chopped

2 celery stalks, chopped

1 cup yellow onion, chopped

3 cups chicken stock or chicken broth

6 tablespoons butter

¼ cup + 2 tablespoons flour

1½ teaspoon salt

Freshly ground pepper to taste

1 cup 2% milk (or unsweetened cashew milk)

½ cup fresh parsley, chopped (optional)

2 cups corn, fresh or frozen

2 cups peas, fresh or frozen

Pie crust, bought or made from scratch

Cook chicken breasts in a skillet and set aside. Cook carrots, celery and onion in the broth covered over medium heat until tender, about 10 minutes. Drain, reserving broth.

Sauce: Melt butter over medium heat. Then add flour, salt and pepper and stir until bubbly. Add reserved broth and milk and bring to a boil stirring constantly until thickened. Add parsley.

Roll out 4 pie crusts and place bottom crusts in the 10-inch pie tins. Add half of the vegetables, cooked chicken and sauce to each pie. Place pie crusts over top and make slits on top. Bake at 375 degrees for 35 minutes or until crust is golden.

Great Aunt Rita's Pie Crust

MAKES 2 CRUSTS (TOP AND BOTTOM)

I LIKE THIS RECIPE BECAUSE IT DOESN'T CONTAIN SHORTENING (AND PARTIALLY HYDROGENATED OILS)

3 cups flour

½ teaspoon salt

1 cup cold butter, cut into ½-inch pieces

1 egg

almost 1 cup milk

Mix flour and salt. Cut in butter pieces and dry ingredients with pastry blender until pea-sized or smaller.

Put egg into measuring cup. Add milk until it reaches the 1 cup line. Beat egg and milk with fork. Then stir it into mixture.

Roll out on a floured surface.

Focaccia with Caramelized Onions and Blue Cheese

SERVES 4–5

Focaccia bread 10–12 inches in diameter or Boboli Italian pizza crust
2–3 handfuls of fresh spinach
1 small onion sliced (about 1 cup)
2 tablespoons olive oil
2½ packed tablespoons dark brown sugar
1–2 tomatoes, sliced
2–3 ounces blue cheese or Gorgonzola cheese, crumbled
1½–2 cups mozzarella cheese

Preheat the oven to 400°F.

Add olive oil to a skillet and place over medium heat. Add sliced onions and brown sugar and caramelize until the onions are translucent and light brown, about 5 minutes. Drain excess liquid.

Next, place focaccia bread on a pizza pan or cookie sheet and layer all of the ingredients onto the bread in this order: spinach, caramelized onion, tomatoes, blue cheese, mozzarella cheese.

Bake for 15–17 minutes, or until the cheese is lightly browned.

Grilled Fish Tacos

SERVES 6

Note: Are you concerned about sustainable fisheries? Check out Monterey Bay Seafood Watch website http://www.seafoodwatch.org/.

1 pound skinless mahi mahi, halibut, or tilapia fillets

¾ teaspoon chili powder

½ cup salsa, divided

2 cups coleslaw mix or shredded cabbage

¼ cup sour cream

¼ cup chopped cilantro, divided

8 (6-inch) tortillas, warmed

Grill fish 8–10 minutes. (Or fry fish in a skillet.) Sprinkle chili powder over fish, then spoon on ¼ cup salsa. Combine coleslaw mix, remaining ¼ cup salsa, sour cream and 2 tablespoons cilantro in a large bowl, mix well.

Slice fish into thin strips, fill warm tortillas with fish, coleslaw mix, and garnish with cilantro.

Herbed Artichoke Chicken

SERVES 6

1½ pounds chicken thighs

2 or 3 tomatoes or 1 (14-ounce) can tomatoes, drained and diced

1 (14-ounce) can artichoke hearts in water, drained

1 small onion, chopped

½ cup pitted Kalamata olives, sliced

1 cup chicken broth

¼ cup dry white wine

3 tablespoons quick-cooking tapioca

2 teaspoons curry powder

1 tablespoon fresh flat-leafed Italian parsley, chopped

1 teaspoon dried sweet basil

1 teaspoon dried thyme

½ teaspoon salt

½ teaspoon black pepper

Combine all ingredients in a slow cooker. Mix. Cook on low for 6–8 hours or on high for 3 ½–4 hours, or until chicken is no longer pink in center.

Lasagna

SERVES 8–10

1 pound ground turkey, bison or beef

1 onion, diced

2 stalks of celery, chopped

6 cups fresh spinach, wilted in frying pan, or 1 (10-ounce) package of frozen spinach

1 (32-ounce) jar spaghetti sauce

1 (32-ounce) container cottage cheese

5 cups mozzarella cheese, one cup reserved

8–10 lasagna noodles, whole wheat recommended

Preheat oven to 350°F

Brown meat in a frying pan. Add chopped onions, celery, and spinach and sauté until onions are translucent. Add spaghetti sauce.

In a separate bowl, combine cottage cheese and mozzarella cheese. In a 9 x 13-inch baking pan, pour half of the meat sauce mixture into the pan and spread evenly. Layer lasagna noodles. Add the cheese mixture on top. Repeat these layers one more time and finish with the reserved mozzarella cheese on top. Cover and bake for 45 minutes. Then remove the cover or aluminium foil and bake for 15 minutes more, or until the cheese browns slightly.

Meat Loaf

SERVES 6

1 pound ground beef
¾ cup quick oats oatmeal
1 egg
1 cup milk
1 small onion, chopped (about ¼ cup)
1 small green pepper, chopped
1 medium carrot, shredded or finely chopped
4 ounces fresh mushrooms, sliced
1 tablespoon Worcestershire sauce
1½ teaspoons salt
½ teaspoon dry mustard
¼ teaspoon pepper
¼ teaspoon rubbed sage
⅛ teaspoon garlic powder
1 tomato, thinly sliced (optional)
4–6 slices of ½ cup shredded cheese (any kind, you choose)

Preheat oven to 350°F.

In a large bowl, combine all ingredients except tomato and cheese. Place mixture into an ungreased bread loaf pan. Bake uncovered for 1–1½ hours or until it is no longer pink inside. You may have to drain the loaf a bit. Top with tomato slices and cheese. Bake until cheese is melted, 3–5 minutes.

Pesto with Pasta

MAKES ABOUT 3 CUPS

8 cups fresh basil leaves (or 8 large handfuls)
½ cup grated Parmesan cheese
¼ cup walnuts or pine nuts
2-3 garlic cloves, peeled
½ teaspoon sea salt
Juice of ½ lemon
¾ cup extra virgin olive oil

Combine all ingredients in a blender or food processor and process until smooth. Serve with pasta or on French bread.

Tip: Freeze pesto in ice cube trays and transfer cubes to a baggy.

Quick Baked Cheese Quesadilla

Serves 6

6 soft tortillas
Extra virgin olive oil
¾ cup sharp white cheddar cheese, grated
½ cup fresh cilantro, chopped
1 cup tomatoes, chopped

You can add other ingredients too: sliced mushrooms, green onions, sliced black olives, chicken, or avocado, to name a few.

Preheat oven to 350°F. Lightly brush a cookie sheet with olive oil. Place the tortillas on the cookie sheet. Cover each tortilla with cheese, cilantro, and tomatoes. Bake for 7–10 minutes, or until the cheese is melted and the tortillas begin to crisp. Fold in half to serve.

Ratatouille

SERVES 4-6

¼ cup olive oil, plus more as needed
1½ cups yellow onion, diced
1 teaspoon garlic, minced
2 cups eggplant, diced with skin on
½ teaspoon fresh thyme leaves
1 cup green bell peppers, diced
1 cup red bell peppers, diced
1 cup zucchini, diced
1 cup yellow squash, diced
1½ cups tomatoes, peeled, seeded and chopped
1 tablespoon basil leaves, thinly sliced
1 tablespoon parsley, chopped
Salt and freshly ground black pepper

Heat a 12-inch saute pan over medium and add the olive oil.

Once hot, add the onions and garlic to the pan. Cook the onions, stirring occasionally, until they are wilted and lightly caramelized, about 5 to 7 minutes.

Add the eggplant and thyme to the pan and continue to cook, stirring occasionally, until the eggplant is partially cooked, about 5 minutes.

Add the green and red peppers, zucchini, and squash and continue to cook for an additional 5 minutes.

Add the tomatoes, basil, parsley, and salt and pepper, to taste, and cook for a final 5 minutes. Stir well to blend and serve either hot or at room temperature.

Rosemary Chicken Gyros

SERVES 6

6 boneless chicken breasts

Salt and pepper

2 tablespoons olive oil

Juice of 1 lemon

¼ cup white wine vinegar

2 garlic cloves, minced

3 tablespoons fresh rosemary, chopped

2 tablespoons fresh basil leaves, chopped

Pita bread

1 cucumber, sliced

1 tomato, diced

1 tablespoon fresh dill, chopped fine

½ cup plain Greek yogurt

Place chicken breasts in casserole dish. Sprinkle with salt and pepper to taste. In a small bowl, combine the olive oil, lemon, white wine vinegar, garlic, rosemary and basil to make the marinade. Pour the sauce over the chicken, coating each piece. Cover the dish and marinate in the refrigerator for at least 4 hours.

Discard the marinade and grill the chicken.

Slice grilled chicken and serve with pitas. Garnish with sliced cucumbers, tomatoes, fresh dill, and Greek yogurt.

Scalloped Potatoes and Ham

SERVES 5–6

10–12 Yukon gold potatoes, sliced into quarter-inch rounds

1 ham steak (about 1½ pounds), cubed (or just put in whole if you don't mind it not being in neat cubes)

1 (10¾-ounces) can condensed cream of mushroom soup

1 soup can of water

3 cups shredded cheddar cheese

Lots of grill seasoning and rosemary to taste.

Combine all ingredients in a slow cooker. Cook on high for 3½ hours, or until potatoes are fork-tender.

Skordalia with Halibut

MAKES 2 CUPS

3 medium potatoes
¼ cup extra virgin olive oil
4 garlic cloves, minced
Juice of ½ lemon
Salt and ground pepper to taste
3 pounds halibut, grouper or other fish
Pita bread

Wash and peel the potatoes before placing them in a sauce pan. Cover with water and boil until the potatoes are cooked and soft. Drain. Transfer the potatoes to a large bowl and mash them with a potato masher. Add the remaining ingredients. Thin with water if needed. Serve with grilled or fried fish and pita bread

Sloppy Joes

SERVES 12

3 pounds lean ground beef

1 cup onion

3 cloves garlic, minced

1¼ cup ketchup

1 red bell pepper, chopped

¼ cup plus 1 tablespoon Worcestershire sauce

¼ cup packed dark brown sugar

3 tablespoons dried mustard

3 tablespoons vinegar

2 teaspoons chili powder

12 toasted hamburger buns

Brown ground beef, onion, and garlic in a skillet over medium-high heat. Drain fat. Combine ketchup, red bell pepper, Worcestershire sauce, sugar, mustard, vinegar, and chili powder in slow cooker. Add beef mixture. Cover and cook on low for 6 to 8 hours. This recipe is great for a party or for freezing since it makes such a big batch.

Thai Chicken

SERVES 6

2½ pounds chicken pieces or thighs. (Note: If you throw them in frozen, they won't dry out)

1 cup medium or hot salsa

¼ cup peanut butter

¼ cup of lime juice (juice of about 2–3 limes)

2 tablespoons soy sauce

2 teaspoons fresh ginger, minced

1½ cups brown or white uncooked rice

½ cup chopped peanuts

2 tablespoon fresh cilantro, chopped

Combine first six ingredients in a slow cooker. Cover and cook on low for 8–9 hours or on high for 3–4 hours (or until chicken is no longer pink in center or 180°F).

Prepare rice as directed on package.

Serve chicken and sauce over rice. Garnish with peanuts and cilantro before serving.

Three-Bean Chili

SERVES 6–8

1 pound ground turkey or beef

1 small onion, chopped

About 3 tomatoes or 1 (28-ounce) can diced tomatoes, undrained

1 cup dried chickpeas (soaked overnight) or 1 (15-ounce) can chickpeas (also called garbanzo beans), rinsed and drained

1 cup dried kidney beans (soaked overnight) or 1 (15-ounce) can kidney beans, rinsed and drained

1 cup dried black beans (soaked overnight) or 1 (15-ounce) can black beans, rinsed and drained

16 ounces tomato sauce

4 ounces diced mild green chilies

1–2 tablespoon chili powder

Brown meat and saute onion in a skillet over medium-high until it is no longer pink. Drain fat. Transfer to a slow cooker. Add remaining ingredients and mix. Cover and cook in a slow-cooker on low for 6–8 hours. If the chili gets too thick, add a little water.

chapter sixteen

Freezing Your Booty

Food Preservation

If you inserted "off" at the end of the chapter title, I am guessing you live in the Midwest. In this chapter I am referring to garden booty, of course. I had grandiose dreams that I would can my bounties so I would have an old-time storehouse of food for the winter. Well, maybe someday, when I have a little more time, I will do this. However, I decided not to cover canning in this book because I decided that it seemed beyond "lawn chair level."

After I had some health issues and was encouraged to stay away from processed foods and refined flours and sugars, I was forced to learn to cook. Now using up what comes from the garden isn't typically a big ordeal and I've also discovered the joys of baggies and vacuum food savers. The basic freezing instructions are: wash, prepare (peel/cut), blanch (boil), cool, bag and seal, freeze. Tomatoes and basil are a bit different. Choose fresh, firm vegetables only and freeze as soon as possible—within 24 hours of picking is ideal. Store them in the refrigerator until you freeze them.

Equipment

- Knife and cutting board
- Large stock pot

- Large slotted spoon
- Big bowl with lots of ice (and more ice on hand to keep adding)
- Vacuum food sealer or plastic freezer bags, such as Ziploc® freezer bags
- Kitchen timer

Freezing Vegetables

Step 1:

Wash (under warm running water—for firm vegetables, use a vegetable scrub brush)

Step 2:

Peel, trim, and cut into smaller pieces

Step 3:

Blanch (boil) according to table on pages 164-165.

All fruits and vegetables contain enzymes and bacteria that, over time, break down and destroy nutrients and change the color, flavor, and texture of food during frozen storage. Blanching in boiling water or steam destroys the enzymes before freezing. The duration is intended to be just long enough to stop the action of the enzymes and kill the bacteria. Blanch time depends on the type and size of the vegetable. Under-blanching stimulates the activity of enzymes and is worse than no blanching. Over-blanching causes loss of flavor, color, vitamins, and minerals.

Place water in a large stock pot and bring it to a rolling boil. Use a gallon of water per pound of vegetables (a pound is approximately two cups of prepared vegetables). Begin counting the blanching time as soon as the water returns to a boil after adding the vegetables. This time should be less than a minute. If it takes longer to boil, vegetables will be soggy. Cover the pot and boil at a high temperature for the required length of time. You may use the same blanching water several times. Be sure to add more water from time to time to keep the water level at the required height.

If you have a steamer, you can use it, but it will usually take 1½ times longer to blanch the food. Steaming works best with broccoli, pumpkin, sweet potatoes, and winter squash. I do not recommend using the microwave because blanching times are longer and it may change the taste and color. Since winter squash keeps for months, I typically just store them whole in my basement over the winter.

Step 4: Cool

As soon as blanching is completed, cool vegetables thoroughly by plunging them in ice water. A properly blanched vegetable is brightly colored all the way through, when sliced with a knife. Cooling vegetables should take the same amount of time as blanching (except corn on the cob).

Step 5: Label, bag, and seal

A vacuum food sealer is a great way to go if you are going to be doing this year after year. Ziploc® bags work, but it is hard to get as much air out of the bags.

Otherwise, you can put a single layer of the vegetable on a shallow pan and put the pan into the freezer. As soon as the vegetable is frozen, put them into a freezer bag or container. Press out air and seal tightly. To me, this is just an extra step that I'd rather not do.

Step 6: Freeze

Twenty-four hours before freezing, set your freezer temperature at -10°F. Only freeze an amount that will freeze solid within 24 hours—this is usually about 2–3 pounds of food per cubic foot. Keep your freezer set at 0°F and use vegetables within 8–12 months for best quality and taste. Always cook frozen vegetables before eating to prevent Listeria monocytogenes. (This is not an issue for fruit because Listeria is not acid-tolerant.) Lay the bags flat if possible.

Freezing Tomatoes

Step 1: Core and Remove Bad Spots

Cut the tomatoes in quarters and remove the tough part around the stem and any bruised or soft parts.

Step 2: Boil to Remove the Tomato Skins

Put the tomatoes in a large pot of boiling water for about 30–45 seconds and then plunge them into a bowl of ice water. The skins will practically slide right off of the tomatoes. (It is important to remove the skins. If you leave the skins on, they become tough, chewy, and discolored.)

Step 3: Cut (optional)

As you're cutting the tomatoes, a lot of water will squeeze out anyhow. If you are planning to make a spaghetti sauce, you may want to squeeze out the seeds and water and drain the tomatoes (you can save the liquid to use for cooking) so the sauce will be thicker.

Step 4: Fill the freezer bags

It's easiest to label and date the bags before filling. Avoid overfilling the bags and try to avoid air pockets. You can use vacuum bags or Ziploc®-type freezer bags. But be sure to squeeze out the extra air.

Step 5: Vacuum seal the bags (if you have a vacuum sealer)

Obviously, if you are not using a vacuum food sealer, just inspect the bags.

Step 6: Freeze the bags.

Store them flat in the freezer.

Freezing Basil

Step 1: Pick the leaves off the stems.

Discard flower buds, stems, and leaves that aren't in good shape.

Step 2: Wash

Step 3: Chop coarsely

Chop by hand, with a food processor or a chopper.

Add 1 tablespoon Fruit-Fresh® produce protector or 1 tablespoon lemon juice per 2 cups packed down basil leaves. (Ball® brand Fruit-Fresh® is available at most grocery stores where canning supplies like pectin and pickling salt are sold. Basically a form of citric acid/vitamin C, Fruit-Fresh® prevents the food from turning brown upon exposure to the air.)

Add ¼ cup extra virgin olive oil per two cups packed down basil leaves. Stuff basil leaves (in small batches) into the food processor and process. Add olive oil and produce protector and process again. The olive oil and produce protector will prevent the basil from turning dark in the freezer.

Step 4: Pack into freezer bags or ice cube trays

Freezer bags work, but I prefer using ice cube rays. I have a few ice cube trays dedicated to freezing pesto and basil. I just freeze it in trays and put the basil or pesto cubes into a baggy after they're frozen. This is a convenient way to store and use it, because most recipes only call for a tablespoon or two of basil. You can just pop a cube or two into your cooking. Freezing in cubes saves you the hassle of wrestling with an unruly chunk of frozen basil just to break off the small piece a recipe requires.

Step 5: Freeze

Be sure to press excess air out of the bags.

Freezing Berries

Step 1: Wash and drain the berries

Rinse the berries gently in cold water. I put a colander or strainer in a large bowl, fill it with cold water and gently swirl the berries in it with my fingers. The debris either floats so I can skim it out, or it sinks and is removed when I lift the strainer out of the bowl.

Step 2: Spread the berries in a pan

There are two ways of doing this. If you have space in your freezer, spread the berries out in a large oven pan with a lip or ridge. Load enough berries onto the pan to make one layer. This method allows the berries to freeze quickly and not be frozen together in a lump. After the berries freeze, transfer them to a sealed container. If your freezer isn't that big, just drain as much of the water as you can and place the berries into whatever container will fit in your freezer. After they are frozen, they may stick together a little bit, but they should break apart fairly easily.

Vegetables	Blanching & Cooling Times (minutes)
Asparagus – small stalk	2
Asparagus – medium stalk	3
Asparagus – large stalk	4
Beans – snap, green, or wax	3
Broccoli (florets 1½ inches across)	3
Broccoli florets – steamed	5
Brussels sprouts – small heads	3
Brussels sprouts – medium heads	4
Brussels sprouts – large heads	5
Cabbage or Chinese cabbage – shredded	1½
Cabbage or Chinese cabbage – wedges	3
Carrots – small, whole	5
Carrots – diced, sliced, or lengthwise strips	2
Cauliflower (florets, 1 inch across)	3
Celery	3
Corn-on-the-cob – small ears	7 (cool for 14 min.)
Corn-on-the-cob – medium ears	9 (cool for 18 min.)
Corn-on-the-cob – large ears	11 (cool for 22 min.)
Corn – whole kernel or cream style (ears blanched before cutting corn from the cob)	4
Eggplant	4
Greens – collards	3
Greens – all other	2
Kohlrabi – whole	3
Kohlrabi – cubes	1
Mushrooms – whole (steamed)	9

Vegetables	Blanching & Cooling Times (minutes)
Mushrooms – buttons or quarters (steamed)	9
Mushrooms – slices (steamed)	5
Parsnips	3
Peas – edible pod	2 to 3
Peas – green	1½ - 2½
Peppers, sweet – halves	5
Peppers, sweet – strips or rings	3
Squash – summer (best if just cooked in a recipe & then frozen)	3
This information is from the U of M Extension http://www1.extension.umn.edu/food-safety/preserving/vegetables-herbs/blanching-vegetables/	

CPSIA information can be obtained at www.ICGtesting.com
Printed in the USA
LVOW11s1913050216

473933LV00007B/39/P